THE NEW CASTLE

Books by Malachi Martin

The Scribal Character of the Dead Sea Scrolls

The Pilgrim (*under the pseudonym, Michael Serafian*)

The Encounter

Three Popes and the Cardinal

Jesus Now

The New Castle

THE NEW CASTLE
Reaching for the Ultimate

MALACHI MARTIN

E. P. DUTTON & CO., INC.   NEW YORK   1974

Short adaptations of the chapters in this book appeared in
Intellectual Digest from October, 1973 through June, 1974.
Copyright © 1973 by Communications/Research/Machines Inc.
Copyright © 1973, 1974 by Ziff-Davis Publications Company
10 9 8 7 6 5 4 3 2 1

Published simultaneously in Canada
by Clarke, Irwin & Company Limited, Toronto and Vancouver

Library of Congress Cataloging in Publication Data

Malachi, Martin.
The new castle; reaching for the ultimate.

1. Religions.   2. Civilization, Modern—1950-
I. Title.
BL80.2.M283   1974   200   74-9663
ISBN 0-525-16553-3

CONTENTS

FOREWORD

The voice is unmistakable. Listen:

Fling a note of music upward. It travels undulatingly
with a life all its own through dome within dome, from
hemicycle to arcade and beyond through unseen corridors
and passages high up in the façades, to still farther corners,
unexpectedly issuing again in solemn arpeggios, speaking to
you as a return message from behind and above and each
side. Standing in the south gallery, you find that you are listening not merely to beautiful acoustics. Some voice is
speaking inside you; and the syllables are translated simultaneously into the movement of the color, shade and the light
above your head. The walls are singing with moving light,
and you are slowly being warmed by some holy fire.

That was the sound of Hagia Sophia in Constantinople. Now, turn westward to the spires of Salisbury, to
the Duomo, to Köln, and through one mind's eye, watch:

We walk between walls that bear no weight but rise up
and dissolve. We have to resist or be taken captive by vertical radiations in arch and line that begin above us, emanat-

ing from the air. Facades become transparencies of colored sunlight. Portals lead inward below successive ribs of molded mastery, drawing us ever farther to the sanctuary and the altar, while growing upward through vast spaces.

And no matter how you try to remain earthbound, the building carries you upward by a simple stratagem: like you, it is part of solid ground, the good earth, but it rises—and takes you with it—to meet a lofty goal. It is your aspiration, you aspiring, in stone. Your desiring self, not measured against an overbearing skyscraper height or a mothering mountain breast, but borne aloft. Your gravity made celestial. And you cannot resist, because it is all done at a human rate of speed: starting slowly with the gravamen of prostrate pavements and feet-deep granite walls and hidden, thrusting foundations in dark crypts; then, unnoticeably, picking up speed with quickening inner details. And, finally, all of the structure—and all inside you, desire, awe, expectation, instinct, curiosity, fear—is gathered up weightlessly, soundlessly spiraling heavenward in a breakneck, never-turning-back bid at the skies above our world.

The voice, the eye, the vision are all one man's. Malachi Martin is remarkable. Take a Celt, a Dublin Celt at that, breed and rear him in the wet mists and fleeting sun of his mysterious native isle, transplant him to the Jesuit enclaves of the Holy City and imbue him with Roman metaphysic, and language, season him for long years under the Italian and other alien suns, then lo, remove him to the New World, to the fever of New York, the languors of the Southeast, the quirky balm of California— and what have you? Only an odd mixture until you add the man, the mind, the spirit, the vaulting prose. You are moving up, on up to other realms, an ascension to the shores of the empyrean. Now, anything becomes possible, including what has been for a half-millennium impossible, a re-synthesis of the physical and metaphysical, of scientific rationality and the reasons of the spirit.

Malachi Martin belongs to a small but growing group

bent on restoring the balance that the West began to lose seven centuries ago when, as he has written earlier, Roger Bacon failed in an effort at persuading the Roman Catholic Church to embrace experimental science. From that terrible rejection came the real schism that has divided the world ever since. With the developing triumph of science, the realm of spirit shrank, slowly, almost imperceptibly at first, and then at an ever-quickening pace from the High Renaissance to the deeps of the twentieth century.

We were enriched beyond human reckoning by the products of the quantifying mind and impoverished, again beyond reckoning, at the same time by what we had lost. Balance was gone, all gone, and we had toppled into a crater of loss and despair to which cartographers of the spirit adapted the name of Kafka.

Only now are we starting the long climb out of the depths of that depression. On our ability to complete the trek depends our survival. If we make it, we will at last have escaped the frustration and defeat of Kafka's *The Castle* to come within sight and reach of the New Castle.

It is the New Castle that is the goal of this extraordinary book by one of the best minds we have on the subject of heaven or hell on earth. The book, in its quest for a new vision of spirit, a new realization of, as Malachi says, "an opening of the divine onto man's affairs," takes us on a journey that begins in Mecca and carries us on to Jerusalem, Constantinople, Rome, Peking, Angkor Wat, Wittenberg and finally, in rightful order, Peru, Indiana. That journey actually started as an idea for a single article for *Intellectual Digest* that turned into a plan for nine articles and for a much expanded book. This book.

Agree with him or not, Malachi Martin is exhilarating, a bubbling embodiment of Bergson's *élan vital*. And since the words here are the man, they have the same quality. To those about to embark on this journey with Malachi, I can say with pleasure: Godspeed. It will be his own kind of anabasis, a march from the coast to the interior, a going up.

Martin Goldman
Intellectual Digest
New York
April 1974

THE NEW CASTLE

I

THE CASTLE

The Castle, as image and expression, is as old as predynastic Egypt and as modern as twentieth-century Europe. Throughout, it has been used to describe human existence on the planet Earth as transformed by a quality which men and women ascribed to something they were sure they instinctively knew, and which time and again they described in terms of spirit. However they defined it ("spirit of man," "the spirit in man," "the spirit of the people"), the Castle for them was a vision in which all the material conditions of human living were invested by "spirit" and thus perfected humanly: time and space no longer as sources or occasions of effort, labor, weight, hindrance, inequality, disease, or death; and their personal lives as set in a dimension of freedom, beauty, light, and love. The Castle was the vision of that ideal state.

In the broad sweep of history, there have been about half a dozen occasions—the outburst of a great religious movement, the apogee of a great culture fathered by such a movement—when, it seemed to masses of men and women, the Castle was within human reach. These happenings were centered in particular cities and countries— Mecca, Jerusalem, Constantinople, Rome, China, Cambodia, Wittenberg, the United States. And they were seen as human thrusts at that humanly perfect quality of existence on Earth; as ascensions of men, by force of the "spirit," to attain the Castle. Human hope and confidence animated each of these thrusts.

In painful contrast, the nadir vision of the Castle was stated by a small handful of men who some fifty years ago at the dawn of our modern day detected the radical shift we all see now in the reality of peoples, cultures, and politics around us, and most pronouncedly within our own geographical and societal confines. Those men saw two main harbingers of that radical shift; and in their nadir vision, the two were seen most often in the dour hues of an ending rather than a beginning. The first of those harbingers is the inexorable mechanization and organization of all human society according to science and technology primarily as developed in the United States. The second is a pervasive dread—somehow connected with mechanization—that the Castle is unattainable or that it exists as nothing more than a dream to torture our days and nights of grim realities. We all share to some degree Franz Kafka's pain and Béla Bartók's tears as they put this doubt into words and set it to music.

Both these men were from central Europe. Both were articulate just when deathlike convulsions sent half the world writhing into the pain, hate, and fear of the First World War. In the twilight of an elitist civilization which had appropriated sociocultural happiness from the masses, placing it on unattainable peaks of blood, rank, and wealth, Kafka described the horror of human impossibility: *The Castle* is the high-placed dwelling unknowable by the simple individual who is the cipher, the human ant among other ants, whose desires and delights would never bed there. Bartók composed music about the horrors of human inevitability: *Duke Bluebeard's Castle* has no windows. And behind each of its seven doors there lies one of man's seven desires slain. Behind the last door, love itself has died by violence.

If, indeed, the pessimism of such men was justified, then the vision of the Castle will have almost ceased for men and women of today. They must renounce any realistic hope of spirit in this world of matter, and forgo any trust that in their humanness they could receive any divine transcendence. They will hug Kierkegaard's bride, human dread, as their only source of greatness, finally succumbing to the death-laden illusion that our humanness is all a product of self creation, and spirit some aberrant chemical reaction in our brains or guts. We will perceive only that human dread. We will not even glimpse the human hope, the striving of our inner and unmeasurable response to new visions. The tinny freshness of modern Jerusalem, the self-cannibalism of Wittenberg's reasoning, the scepticized lines of human beings in Ko Kung, and the linear nudity of Peru, Indiana can then, each in its own way, awake us to our own existence only as aerated things and to our own destiny only as the product of protean powers we cannot ultimately control and that can only let us die, each one. The rest, the building blocks of the Castle, the new Castle itself, and all transcendence, all hope beyond wishing for another day of drudging, grudging life will be lost to any sight of ours.

However, a journey to the human sites of ancient ascensions gives us to understand (without forcing our assent) that the awesome shift in human affairs today is due to the ceaseless leavening and continual working of spirit in man. We are clambering out from the hard literal surfaces where men's theories and ambitions imprisoned us.

A new Castle is prefigured. As the old, it lies beyond the measure and microscope of science and the caliper of reason. But it reveals a human reason for science and makes all human reasoning worthwhile.

The journey to the Castle, the effort and ascension to attain it, is the most human and the least cerebral of all mankind's journeys. The first definitive move Castle-ward within us happens in an atmosphere which, we find, is not in any part of our memories: on a soil with fragrances not of flowers, with colors not of our carnality, with steps not of space, and tones not of time. We are urged on that journey, not as many are to the Vale of Kashmir or the islands of Greece by that half-sensual, half-mental curiosity known to every experienced traveler. Least of all are we ever motivated by the calculating eagerness and self-satisfaction of the "intellectual." It is no pilgrimage of the mind, no trip in the machine of logic, no safari of research. Rather, it is an opening to the spirit.

Any man's opening to the spirit encounters two difficulties at the outset. First, the clinging tendency to imagine spirit as something roaming around in empty inaccessible voids, and ourselves as separate, as vibrant, breathing mosaics of living bodies, thinking minds, desiring hands, working fingers, walking feet, as merely pragmatic and solid beings breathing and dying in cities and in lands around the face of the globe. In thrall to this tendency of thought, steamy words are written and spoken for and against spirit (not only by quack metaphysicians); and as reasonable men we half wish for, and half scoff at, the reality of spirit in our human lives.

Second, because the vision of Castle is old in humanity, we carry within us the desires of many to reach the Castle. Throughout our lives, we walk with a ghostly multitude, companions from all our pasts, faces known and unknown, those who went before us and made us humanly possible, the commensals of our cultural selves. Their impatience is our legacy from them; and it animates our feet and eyes. In their lore, in their letters, in treasured memories of their words, and perhaps in other less understood ways, they are always there, seemingly. Our "familiars." But, while they may have guided us to the antechamber of our longings, they can only freeze at the door. We respond to the dreams they dreamed before us. We look backward in order to follow the direction of their pointing fingers. But in the lurch of our encounter with the Castle's vision, they all leave us. The Castle is of the living; and we can perceive it only at living moments.

All hindrances notwithstanding, there are during our lives break points in the flow of each one's consciousness: moments of knowledge which are neither logical nor rational nor irrational, but prelogical and prerational. At such a break point, we always see the Castle, the momentarily stock-still vision of our human wishes become beautiful and serene as on a pinnacle, gleaming in our very recognition of it; shimmering with a promise. Unless we heighten our awareness, the break point slips past us like mercury. Almost immediately, the moment is over. We plunge weighted by sorrow or joy, pain or pleasure, revulsion or desire, resolution or conclusion. And thus our impression is of consciousness as an unbroken line. Nevertheless, in the reality of our days and nights, we frequently live that variable moment of fleet fracture: a point where human thoughts cease and before our human emotions begin. It is our only genuine instant of intuition. We make no effort— nor are we impelled—to think; neither has any emotion flooded us, calling for submersion in it or control over it. It is the *occasion* of each person's opening to spirit.

The break point is momentary. But while it lasts, there is exhilaration, a weightlessness of the human self launched by thought, an instant when our innerliness is clear and untrammeled: when a child smiles and just before we smile in return; when a friend dies and just before we realize that we still live on; when the sight of something beautiful fills our eyes—the Blue Mosque in Constantinople; or when we see something great—the lift-off of a Saturn rocket, or something venerable—the body of a dead hero; and it is always just before we react spontaneously.

At such moments, the Castle appears in all its personal force: our fate as separate and distinct individuals seems to reside there. The Castle for us is the consummation of all deepest wishes: for that fleeting time there is no waiting any longer, no limit to daylight, no fears in the night, no further clogging of body or brain, no shadows; we are together; we are unique. All is well. Fully well. And we never see ourselves in the Castle as alone either from other people—all human beings—or from this human world of ours. But this coming-togetherness and being-togetherness, in spite of verbal appearances, is not classified by us under any sociological or political or cultural category. These are the handy tags of the brain; whereas the Castle is a vision that arises within us: it appears as the answer to the warp and woof of our innerliness; yet we know it to be distinct from us.

The central promise of the Castle and our spontaneous recognition of it are always intricately woven together. The Castle has always been the point where human life, merely brimful of its exigencies and weights, has encountered the human vision of its own worth and meaning. Its promise has always seemed to men and women to concern freedom from the heaviness of bodily life that lies upon each one, but not the cessation of that bodily life.

For a human life, no matter what health it enjoyed, or what sunlit days it included or what success it brought, or what freedom it entailed, seemed to be tied to the earth—

by the burden of time to be passed and space to be covered; by the hindrance of illness, disease, injury, or insanity; by the pack of poverty on a man's back; by the dead load of increasing years and old age; and, finally, by our return as dust to that earth. But the Castle always promised to free us from the weight of humanness in each one, yet to preserve that humanness and, indeed, to embellish it with freedom and impunity. Once the Castle was attained, men imagined, their bodies would share in the freedom their minds and wills already enjoyed.

It is not surprising then that, as the ideal human state, the Castle, in reflection and in clever brains, can be (and has frequently been) confused with well-known elements: heaven of religions, Utopia of Idealists, Millennium of political heroes, Nirvana of Buddhists, Celtic Isles of the Blest, Asphodel Paradise of Dorians, Valhalla of Vikings. It is none of these things, of course; and yet it is reflected in them all. It is heaven. But not heaven in Heaven. Not heaven Heaven. It is heaven on our human Earth. And generations have thought of Castle as heaven on Earth.

As living ideal, it shares its properties with daily reality. It has height, distance, weight, perpetuity, and the human smile. It has reason and the security of the forbidden. It is in linear connection with ultimate blessedness. With Heaven. And, therefore, as prime quality, it offers immediacy of what would otherwise be as remote as Atlantis. Its inhabitants are cheek-to-cheek with beauty itself, with repose itself, with truth. In finality. In lastingness. In it, men and women would find regnancy of being but indulge in no grandezza of pride. They might never return "home" but would suffer no nostalgia. They would retain desire but have no inner ache. And, according to its vision, men would be able to overleap, to transcend all physical barriers.

And this appears to be the human ideal: transcendence, an imponderable condition of human being. That transcendence is the very atmosphere of the Castle: a unique light in which the Castle stands before us in the wordlessness of our first recognition, defying any Kafka-esque vision of human fate. In a way we cannot compre-hend, we find that light to be of unflecked brightness and to be ceaseless. It dawns on us for the first time that light can clothe mystery—no shadows are required; and sud-denly in the uniqueness of that light we see that both the perspective of objects and the distances between identifia-ble coordinates have nothing to do with ceaselessness—rather, such things mark the limits of cease.

We find it to be a light which the eye has never seen: unspeakably bright but not glaring, unspeakably soft but not dim. Within it, spirit and matter are wound as a veil wraps gently around the body that is desired and the eye that desires: each detail dwells in clarity, and the whole is ceaselessly familiar and unendingly mysterious. It is se-vere, because it precludes reverie. It is dry and bare of all verbal expression because it brooks no language. Yet, as soon as we perceive it, nothing seems more natural to us; nothing richer, nothing more refreshing, nothing more love filled. And although we may never have perceived it before, we now realize that all along we carried around with us the ability to perceive it, as a diamond which could not be crushed by the crassness of our mistakes and fumblings, or by the weight of all our gangling efforts to succeed as individuals.

One characteristic of the Castle is always underlined by those who genuinely perceive it and report about it: it owes nothing to any particular race of men, group of indi-viduals, individual man or woman; rather, it is the object of all humankind and in that sense belongs to all—in-dividually and collectively. But (there's the rub), while it is perceived in its totality, it comes in time and in each particular place to be expressed fragmentarily. Whole as each vision may be in the instant of opening to spirit, each attempt to tell the vision breaks into parts under the weight of words. For human expressions (words, actions, images, symbols, thoughts) are all particular and limited. All take on the shape of culture, are tied with the strings of syntax, reflect the hues of schools of logic that filter into and color every effort to share unfettered vision.

But most basically and most importantly among men and women until now, diversity in expression of vision of the Castle was assured by the most ancient circumstance of human being: the dependence of humanness on the land which each man and woman inhabited. From the most ancient times, men and women had what we can accurately call an unsigned covenant with their lands: those lands would provide the fabrics to clothe not only their bodies but their very humanness. Different accents were orchestrated as aural portraits of the lands where they echoed. Thoughts, emotions, symbols, loyalties, and the very meaning attributed to human existence seemed hard or soft, jagged or flowing, according to the land from which they sprang. Each land was thus humanly articulated through its inhabitants, its landsmen and landswomen; and each man and woman was a living articulation of that land.

Such fragmentation of expression was spread not merely across space, but through time. It was the Castle's height that was anciently measured in Jerusalem: Heaven was seen touching Earth there. Its light was seen once and for all on Patmos: all the luminosity of living which the Greeks taught men shone there, and is forever pictured in Constantinople. Its perpetuity in eternal calm, its *pax romana*, are mirrored in Rome: men go there and get no taste of death—as they do in all of man's other great cities. The smile of its beauty is indestructible at Angkor Wat. Its distance from the groveling past is drawn in Ko Kung, the Forbidden City of Pekin, the unattainable. Its reason was insistently claimed at Wittenberg: "We would understand," they hammered at the heavy doors of opaque mystery and the stiffness of panoply; "there must be reason." Linear continuation of the Castle with Heaven configures Peru, Indiana: the square of its shopping center, the straight line of Main Street, the right angle of Grant and West Fifth, the honeycomb of Washington Avenue take on the function of symbols here. And in Mecca, Saudi Arabia, men first lived the immediacy of the spirit as the air to be breathed.

A physical revisiting of those sites of ancient vision must, in its own way, be an ascension of the mind. By means of the fragmented expression men achieved at each place, we must intuit the whole, stepping as through a looking glass within the total vision to which men once ascended there. Otherwise, we will return with a mere travelog but be enriched with no meaning. Nor must we stop at the lineaments of the Castle as anciently perceived. This would be merely to exercise the cooling embers of reason on the dead past but be warmed at no vision. Besides, this would defeat the whole purpose of a revisiting: to delineate something of the new vision of the Castle as men today express it desiringly and hopefully. For, in the final analysis, why such an undertaking as a revisiting of the Castle if not to catch a glimpse of our latter-day analog?

There is one most puzzling question to answer as we travel. Throughout nations and continents today, there is a perceptible stirring of peoples, each one away from the thoughts, symbols, emotions, myths, celebrations of their land, away from the ancient articulation of the land through them. Their present no longer flows from their past; rather, it meets it in violent confrontation. Clearly, the mechanization will proceed—nothing imaginable can stop that. And, in like measure, men and women are moving away from all fragmented expression of that vision which originally was received whole and entire: the vision of the Castle. Standing at the center of this vast change, Americans are now asking the questions which will be asked over and over again far beyond their country's shores. Without the hint of a smile or any responding jokes, they wonder if this is Mach 1 of Armageddon.

Has all vision of the Castle, then, ceased, throttled by our dreadful doubtings, done to death by the unsettling change in human life? If so, we will encounter only wan ghosts in the sand that whips around the Cobbler's Arch in Mecca, among the starlings that nest noisily on the Appian Way, among the peaceful ruins of Angkor Wat, by the Golden Horn of Constantinople. Ghosts and silent epitaphs.

Or has a new vision of the human Castle already begun to appear? Not induced by philosophers, theologians, social scientists, novelists, dramatists. But born (as are all life-giving visions) into the consciousness of men and women and itself as yet nameless and faceless; but drawing us on through all our painful fractures and dislocations because, as of old and as it always will be in a human world, our humanness is our sure guarantee of a divine preference.

MECCA
Immediacy of Spirit

The heart of Islam is housed in the heart of Mecca: a rectangular cube of a building, 40 by 35 by 50 feet, draped in a black brocade with inwoven gold lettering. *No god but Allah. And Mohammed, his Prophet.* The Kaaba. Its four corners point to the four points of the compass. Outside, in the eastern corner, a fragmented black stone about eleven inches in diameter, held together by a silver band and a ring of stone, polished by the kisses of pilgrims since the eighth century. No windows. Only a door seven feet from the ground in the northeast wall. Inside the Kaaba, really nothing. Three pillars to support the roof in velvet darkness. Silver and gold hanging lamps. Flickering shadows redolent of incense and men's hopes. And the silence. "Hear me!", the Kaaba states wordlessly. "Hear me! Hear me say more than you can ever hear." More than a Western mind can take. The ever more we associate with vastness.

Outside the Kaaba, you look up at the Minarets of Al-Ahram, your eye measuring their height over against the distant radio station pylon and the Hill of Lastingness. You move over to the Wall of Seeing. To the north, Jebel el Nour. To the south, Jebel Thor. Between them, a third mountain, Abu Qubais. At its foot stands the house where Mohammed was born. The Prophet.

Mecca appears to be swaddled in greatness. Mountains around its streets. Deserts around the mountains. And endless sky above the deserts. An endlessly visible horizon around the sky. An unbroken silence pouring into it from all sides. Winds blowing unendingly across it from the deserts and on over more deserts. There is, to be sure, profusion of detail in color and form, much variation of light and shadow. But houses, animals, streets, people, the sounds of Arabic, the traffic—every detail seems to swim, yet not be drowned, in some invisible ether of vastness opening on to unseen light, unmeasured distance, unheard sounds, most beautiful strangeness. It is that very vastness, though invisible, which is articulated in the words, the faces, the colors, the clothes, the gestures, the very dust of this place. It is all around. Immediate. Present. At midday, the muezzin chants God's message from the minaret: "We are nearer to a man than his jugular vein. . . . When I love him, I am the hearing he hears with, the sight he sees with, and the hand he strikes with, and the foot he walks with . . ."

In Mecca, native and visitor alike stand where once the apparently impossible took place and where the air is still quickened by its effect. Here, some time in the early seventh century A.D., men and women experienced the spirit in total *immediacy*. It was a powerful experience, and involved a vision of the human Castle unparalleled in human history. They called the vision Islam (Submission) and themselves Muslims (the Submissive Ones). With that immediacy as inspiration, with spirit as companion, and a vision of the human Castle as a part of all their vistas, they poured out across Arabia, spilling over into Europe, Asia, and Africa. By 715 A.D., less than one hundred years later, against all but the insanest odds, they possessed an empire which stretched from Spain in the west to the Ganges of India. To paraphrase Octavio Paz, they had seen the human world on God's palm, and they named that moment Perfection of the Finite. "You ride for Paradise, O Muslims," wrote the Prophet. "Believers! Make Paradise here. Believers! Die and live in Paradise for the eternal now." And they rode out, and they touched five of the seven seas.

Everywhere they rode, they threw up the physical signs of their vision of Castle, their pale earthly hints of what Paradise might hold, symbols of a desert people: fountains plentiful with cool running water; green, waving palm trees; blossoming rose, jasmine, lily, columbine; shaded rooms, colonnaded porticoes. And everywhere: their buildings as an eloquent physical expression of their knowledge of Castle. The flaunting arches streaking with earth colors. The forests of intricately chiseled columns. The shade and splash of cool light echoed in the sound of sparkling water. And the arabesque. Everywhere, the arabesque, as *signature of spirit*. The central design extending in curved, angular, straight patterns that in turn generate stars within circles, squares within stars, flowers and fruit and beads linked by fragile stems and stout columns and intertwining twigs that flow into Arabic lettering ("No god but Allah. Mohammed, Allah's Prophet.") and double back to rejoin and repeat the central design. Color, rhythm, and form tumble and twine in symmetries leading to the asymmetrical. Visual and tactile traceries taper into invisible tracks and then give on to farther traceries. Semicircles bud unexpectedly from the sides of squares. Curves interrupted by jagged points flow into empty spaces, to reappear beyond in aery ellipses as in epigrams of mystery.

The Western eye at first sees no arabesque here but an intricate design to be studied in each detail; the Western mind will begin by snapping like a camera, recording lines, forms, details. Snap. Snap.

To a point, that mind can understand by parallel: the arabesque is to Islam what the statue was for the Greeks, the oil painting for the men of the Renaissance, and classical music for the belle époque of the nineteenth century: the cameo vision of the perfectly human, of the humanly perfect. But only to a point. And in that point of departure is marked the difference between the Islamic vision and the Western mind that would know and perhaps share it.

The Muslim mind does not record the detailed forms. There is no snap snap. There is the perception rather of the subtle viscous light wafting at all corners, deepening angles, melting intricacy. Beyond gleams sand, sky. Even as the light comes from beyond the traceries, so the vision is deeper than the eye; it attends to the beat of our own inwardness; it weaves all into a see-through lattice for your spirit to commune with spirit. Arabesque becomes see-through mirror; arabesque invites you to look not *at*, but *through* and *beyond;* arabesque stands as symbol of all reality.

Things, all things, should be images in this way: *through* them you should be able to reach for what they image. Not *in* them, for then they are only opaque again, are merely things in themselves, ending any further vision. And not *because* of them, for then they are links in a logical chain, conclusions in themselves, at best part of a syllogism. But *through* them. All the while they remain as things through which you see, think, know.

All of this may seem aery-faery to our Western minds. It is alien. Such perception is a strain, not a vision. For the men of the West, in our quest for knowledge—our own search for vision—made the greatest abstraction from reality: matter.

In the concept of matter, we fitted the external world to our minds as a shoe to the foot. But the shoe is never part of the foot. We create a fiction in two dimensions, spatializing time and chronologizing space; and then we move within it as our only reality. Outside that fiction we are lost. Inside it, reality becomes a mental construct, reduced to what is measurable. And reality is swallowed into the fiction where the intangible becomes unreal, mystery becomes merely puzzle, we cannot perceive the inalterable physiognomies of spirit or see-through lineaments of human life which together make life human. The constants of human being escape us. Even the professional believers among us have tied the spirit with mind-forged manacles—the Aristotelian syllogism, the Roman formulary, the factualized hypothesis cast in scientifically acceptable terms.

But however aery-faery and nonsensical for the Western mind the see-through vision and immediacy of spirit, there is one fact that must engage even the mind caught in the abstraction of matter: with that vision and immediacy only, with no logically compelling ideology, no political instruction, no religious dogma, no hard-headed assessment of the forces ranged against them in the Persian and Byzantine empires—the twin colossi of that day which they overthrew—Muslims traveled and conquered, introducing something vivid and of a new dimension throughout a vast area. Eastward and up through what now are Syria, Lebanon, Iraq, Iran, Pakistan, Afghanistan, Turkey, across India, and down to Indonesia. Westward across Africa, through the Sudan, Egypt, Libya,

Tunis, Morocco, Algeria. Across the Mediterranean to Gibraltar, up through Spain, into France.

Nor can we explain this onrush by some facile modern concept as the desire for *Lebensraum*. They were in another condition. Not a social framework (though, as with any people who spring from any land, expression takes on the colorations and contours of place). Not so much either a condition of mind. Rather, a state of consciousness, that which impelled them outward to proclaim everywhere the condition of spirit that made their enterprise possible. About that state they were very explicit. At one moment, they said, they were all merely men and women. Land bound. Mecca bound. Time bound. Tribe bound. Desert bound. Flesh bound. Space bound. Death bound. Merchants. Bedouins. Laborers. Artisans. Masters. Slaves. Mortals all. Suddenly, they had become other. Their human lives were invaded. A new condition had been created and in it their human condition was completely and palpably changed. Spirit was come. Was present to them. Immediate to them. They accepted. They submitted. The Submissive Ones: Muslims. Their Submission: Islam.

This presence, this immediacy of spirit they took as the prime condition of their humanness. Because of it, they said, they became genuinely human. Before that, they had been mere "clots of blood and flesh and muscle," nearer to animals than human. Now, so human were they because of spirit that they knew the name of spirit: Allah. Time and space were *humanized*. Time past was not lost. Time present did not pass. Time future was here. All time was redeemed from nothingness by the unchanging presentness of spirit. Space and all it contained or conveyed— smell, taste, touch, sound, length, height, color, hard, soft—all was understood to be human and real in its dimensionality: not *because* it had dimensions, but because the nondimensional made dimensions a possibility; not *because* it could be measured, but because it was included in the immeasurable.

Make no mistake. In all this, in the spirit of Islam, in the quality and essence of that vision of the Castle, in the immediacy and presence of spirit, matter was not wiped out or neglected. There was no "amputation" of matter analogous to the Western "amputation" of that which is not matter. Nor was it merely, as Western humanists had imagined, that some soul of beauty was perceptible through the forms of matter. All matter assumed a grandeur from the circumambient spirit. There was no "divine leakage" from Heaven into this universe. Rather, an investment of the physical universe by the divine as a condition of being human.

At one moment—about the year 1000 A.D. as a cliché date, Islam and Christianity had arrived at the same crossroads. For a brief period, they almost decided to travel together. It happened in one area: the south of France and the northern half of Spain. Prior to the Muslim conquests, the area had been thoroughly Christianized since the second century. Five centuries later, Spain and southern France had received a flood of Jewish scholars, themselves fleeing Babylonia before the Muslim armies and bringing with them a tradition of mystic prayer and knowledge of the spirit which they had maintained and developed unbroken since the fifth century before Jesus. And finally, the Muslims, sweeping over the area, leavening it with their Islam. Even when Charles Martel broke their armies at Tours in 732 A.D., their Islam remained; some new force had been let loose in the area. It was a ripe time. The Christians had not yet taken to philosophy: God, Jesus, salvation, man and woman, none of Christianity had been encased in a syllogism. The inquisitive men at Oxford, Cambridge, and Paris were only beginning to guess at the value of positive knowledge. Scientific method and scientific defensiveness were still remote. Muslim and Christian had not yet been bloodied by the Crusades.

Within that small area of meeting and over the space of some few decades, there was for the first and last time in 3000 years of Western history an efflorescence of acquaintance with spirit, immediate and living, as man's cardinal value. In the yearning for such a moment, Isaiah in eighth-century Jerusalem and Diogenes in fourth-century Athens had gone barefoot and naked for three years. But it was here; and it was a commingling. The transcendence of Jews beyond history and mortality; the compassion of Christians who believed in love born of a woman for mankind's sake; the submission of Muslims to the force of the spirit. A brief moment shared by a few in the billions of years of Earth's existence. Islam's finest hour, in which both Christians and Jews learned from Muslims how to walk in their universe as beside a see-through lattice giving on to present divinity.

We who now read their writings and examine their way of life find it hard to see and understand what they did. All life and the whole of life was told by them as an arabesque of human perception. Their thought and language reflect a consciousness riven through with myriad dovetailing imagery. There was no leaping over dense barriers to a lonely frontier of human exploration. No "reaching out," no "filtering through," no searching of light "from," no "at last" moment, no transit between two interpenetrating gyres. It was as if air became visible: you still went on breathing. Just as its immediacy or immediateness is realized, only because it *is* immediate, is not "beyond" anything, never came "from" anywhere, is its own confirming epiphany. Reading those writings as they were written, you are not roaming "timelessly" with the spirit in a new space. You are living in its plenum. You always did. But you never knew it as immediate.

The finest Christian expression to flow from this experience came only after Christianity and Islam decided to travel separate roads. John of the Cross and Teresa of Avila were direct heirs of the ancient tradition. They were the first in Christianity's history to intuit and formulate the steps whereby a worshiper of Jesus of Nazareth could find the divine in the human because Jesus was God and man. In the meantime, profound changes had affected Europe and the Middle East. By the opening of the fifteenth century, deep fissures appeared in the structure Islam had built. Empire politics, dynastic rivalries, local jealousies, Asiatic invasions, the Crusades, the departure of Muslims from Spain in 1492, all were symptoms of a new world aborning. By the end of the fifteenth century, an invisible wall separated Christians and Muslims.

The damage was deep. Islam was not only cut off from the development of thought and empirical experimentation of the West. Its own original thrust at purity was turned aside by the advent of Asiatic Othmans, founders of the Turkish Ottoman Empire. The Castle as envisoned by the early Muslims became identified with an empire which admittedly escaped no human weakness or corruption known to us from the long spotted history of human imperialisms. Not until the twentieth century were the lands of Islam freed from Ottomanism. By that time, Islam outside Arabia had been diluted with as many nationalisms as there are Muslim countries and governments. Arabia itself, since the end of World War I, has been a kingdom ruled by the Saudi royal house.

Now in Mecca of today and throughout the Saudi Arabia of the waning twentieth century, the Muslim vision of Castle quickens. It is not lost. But it is moving Muslims differently now. And it involves a great gamble. The

Saudis are acutely aware of that gamble, just as they were
at an earlier time explicit about that special state of consciousness which led them out of Mecca and across the
world. Briefly it is this: can Muslims adopt and make their
own the science and the technology of the West and—far
from damaging or limiting their vision of the Castle—in-
stall that vision within the hand-crafted, science-created
lanes and structures of postindustrial human habitation?
For the Muslims bid fair to achieve a technotronically conditioned society before most of Europe and much of
America. Willy-nilly, Muslims have been forced into this
gamble by something expressed in three letters: o-i-l. Arabia is today pouring not armies, but "black gold" out of
the desert. By 1980, the annual revenue for the total population of the area around the Arabian Gulf (approximately
twenty-five million people) will be in excess of fifty billion
dollars. Now this Muslim society is committed, as definitively as an arrow which has just left the bowman's hand,
to changing their human habitat with the linear structures,
the faceless power stations, and the mechanized units
which only science and technology can supply.

    And the change is already well under way: jet planes
in the skies; an ultramodern airport in every major city;
modern ports for deep sea-going ships; an intricate communications system; radio and television as part of daily
life; tarmac roads, dams, reservoirs, desalination projects;
deserts blooming with fruit gardens, vegetable farms,
fields of grain, meadow land, trees, flowers, and lawns;
huge mining projects and agricultural projects; cities and
towns with boulevards, paved streets, skyscrapers, apartment buildings, private houses, clinics, schools, technical
institutes, universities, bookshops, supermarkets, and factories; no starvation, no real poverty, disease being eliminated, nutrition standards higher than in parts of Europe
and the United States. At Dhahran, Riyadh, Jeddah, and

elsewhere, the same subjects are taught as in Paris, New York, London, Marseilles. At all major Western centers, Arabians graduate every year in electronics, architecture, medicine, astronomy, mathematics, geology, dentistry—all our Western branches. The Bedouins, nomads in this area for over 5000 years, are being settled. Running water, plumbing, shops, medical attention, radio and television, frozen food, fresh vegetables, permanent houses, mechanical transport, education—these are changing fundamentally an age-old life style.

Still, the same Islam is infusing their minds as transfused the mud brick house from which Mohammed went to preach his message twelve centuries ago: submission of men and women to the felt reality and acknowledged immediacy of spirit in the human condition. All that they are now acquiring by way of modernization and technology as well as science for their minds, all this complex grid of the man-made is understood by them as a novel and intricate arabesque imposed on physical reality, through which there still invisibly wafts the total human reality only guaranteed by spirit. Like looking at a star head on, not to the left or right. Its headlong brightness corridoring a world within, without, and beyond. You are a stethoscope, all of you, listening to the high harmonics of a material universe which has been made human because the divine has chosen what is human. And if, as fearful children of our logic, we protest spontaneously: "How can I know what I think, until I hear what I say?", the small voice of truth admonishes: "Say no word. Think no name. Just see. Just know."

What did we in the West do that they, Muslims, can do otherwise? We know what choice we made: somewhere between 1000 and 1600 A.D., men in the West decided (it was an explicit judgment) that the final outpost of human reality was to be attained only by factual knowledge, scientific experience, objective verification, and technological application. Indubitably it followed: spirit is not included in our reality. We saw it simplistically: "Either you *say* God is in this test tube, or you go ahead anyway and analyze its contents and ignore the other problem." We thus have gained huge and minutely accurate control of our physical universe. But, in so doing, we seem to have fallen outside the reality of our humanness. We placed some of mankind's most brilliant achievements in the universe off limits to the spirit. And we hurt. Somewhere deep down, we are hurting.

The Muslim gamble has simple choices: either the stuff of science and technology will become the new arabesque of meaning, or it will oppress and become for Muslims an opaque wall separating them from their Castle.

In central Mecca, you walk across the Square of the Obedient, down by the Prophet's Lane, and you stop beneath the Cobbler's Arch where a children's game is in progress. Hopscotch of a kind. A child is jumping one leggedly from square to square on the inner edge of a circle. A repeated jingle: "Allah sees! You live! Allah sees! You live!"—for each faultless jump. But: "Allah sees! You, nothing! Allah sees! You, nothing!"—for each fall outside the circle of reality.

3

JERUSALEM
Chosen Place

Monday evening June 5, 1967. Old Jerusalem, manned by 5000 Jordanians, is tightly surrounded by three Israeli brigades with automatic weapons. The end is a matter of time. And force. Israeli aircraft have napalmed all defense outposts. The Church of St. John and the Al-Aqsa Mosque have been strafed. By Tuesday evening, the Israelis are inside the city. It is total surrender. The first Israeli control units almost frantically make their way eastward to a small open patch of ground, 120 feet square, backed by a section of wall. *The* wall. An Israeli paratrooper, his Uzi gun slung over his shoulder, the stains and dust of battle still on his clothes, leans against the wall, both hands raised above his head with the palms touching the worn faces of the stones. He is crying. And whispering: "Blessed be the Lord of Israel, Creator of the Skies and of the Earth." These are no tears of sorrow. Or of pain. Not even of triumph and victory. They are tears of expectation, of *reaching*. He is joined by others.

Visually, that wall is a hybrid: nineteen layers of huge

stone blocks hidden beneath the ground and resting on the
rock bottom of the Tyropean Valley; from the ground up,
nine rows of the same monoliths—twenty-eight rows were
placed there by King Herod as part of the Second Temple, sometime in the last century before Jesus; on top of
them, four rows of smaller stones added by the Romans
three centuries later, and crowned with several more
layers added by the Muslims between 700 and 1200 A.D.
The wall, the Wailing Wall, is the only visible and touchable remnant of the Jerusalem which Jews once possessed,
and definitively lost, 1932 years previously.

An army chaplain mutters the words of Jacob, given in
the Bible: "This is the House of Elohim and the Gate of
the Skies." But this is for want of words. None here are
reaching for the Temple of Herod. Or for any shrine. It is
not a matter of religion. Or of nationalism. They are
reaching for the beauty that once reigned in their Jerusalem, for the vision of the Castle once seen there in that
beauty. Here, Heaven was seen touching Earth. For once,
men and women measured, in the very human terms of
time and place, the height of human perfection as ideally
enshrined in Heaven. Elsewhere, that height remained inaccessible and unmeasurable. But here it made the mountain of Jerusalem and its people chosen forever, searing a
vision of the human Castle into the Jewish soul. That Jewish face of beauty has been veiled in multiple exiles of
heart, of mind, of spirit, of body. Exiles of almost 2000
years. Now, at this moment, no Talmud matters. Nor
Torah nor Synagogue. Nor Rabbi nor Menorah. Nor Midrash nor Piyyut. Nor Shabbas nor Shul. These have all
become veils. Even the traditional weeping and wailing at
the Wall have become a veil over that beauty. And, although no Jew alive today has ever known that beauty, the
Jewish heart has never been able to forget the syllables
with which it told its choice of Jews: "Never shall you see

beauty, except in Zion. Never shall you have life, save in Jerusalem."

Thus they reach today, the paratrooper, the army chaplain, for the Castle in an old vision made new. They stand at the head of a procession as long as the lives of all Jews exiled from the Castle. This is a kernel moment of history which kaleidoscopes the space of four continents and the time of thirty centuries. This evening of June 6 is a zoom instant in which we focus a close-up scrutiny on the little group by the Wall.

But that group diminishes in size, the horizon widens, as the camera of our seeing draws back and recedes into space, into past time, helter-skelter and dizzyingly over waters, lands, cities, centuries, tracing the long line of those who reached out through the bonds of mortality, who spent all their lives reaching out. Through the barbed wire at Dachau, Auschwitz, Belsen, and the bars of the cattle trains of the 1940s. Through the steerage gratings of immigrant ships bound for America in the nineteenth century. Through the criss-crossing roadlets and alleys of staedtls in central Europe during a thousand years. Up through the huddled anonymities of centuries. A forest of unknown hands reaching out of ghetto darknesses, Good Friday massacres, periodic pogroms, flames and fires, forgotten temples, momentary Sabbath peace, Roman prisons, Alexander's armies, Persian occupation, Egyptian invasion, Assyrian siege, Philistine oppression. Back to David, the shepherd king. And back beyond him. Into the shadowy centuries of the second millennium before the wall was built.

This is the procession of reachers, as far back as it goes; the line of Jews aiming at their Castle, that began when Abraham was Abram in Ur of the Chaldees, when men wrote letters on mud tablets, iron was unknown as a metal, and Jerusalem was merely a flat mountain ledge dedicated to Salem, the all-high god.

Abraham, an obscure Semite nomad of towering stature, was the head of the long family, the first witness of the Jewish vision. He is memorialized as father and exemplar of living Jewish faith at grips with history and with its eternal ruler. For some brief chapters in the book of Genesis, the veils of history are drawn aside; he stalks across the scene as the unshakable patriarch of Judaism's far beginnings: we barely learn of his success when he disappears again into the cloud of unknowing. We learn that he believed because of sheer belief, that he steadfastly underwent the *contest* of his *hope:* in the shadow of Jerusalem, fate handed him a live coal and he held it beneath his armpit without wincing or crying out. For his trust in the All High and his hope in history, he entered permanently into human history as the father of perpetual generations.

Jacob, his grandson, was the second witness and the Ulysses of Judaism: crafty, married to a much-loved wife, protected by a special blessing. On one of his journeys, Jacob slept at Bethel, some miles from Jerusalem, and dreamed. He saw a ladder stretching from the earth "to the top of the skies." On it, the angels of his god were ascending and descending from earth to sky and from sky to earth. And his god reiterated the promise of racial perpetuity and security made formerly to his grandfather. When Jacob woke, he realized the beauty revealed: "This," he said to himself, his sight falling upon the familiar land around him, "this is the House of Elohim and the Gate of the Skies." The place of the Castle.

The two witnesses of the ancient vision had been dead and gone for at least five centuries when their descendants and the carriers of the vision, the Jews, swung into the full light of history in the eleventh to the tenth centuries B.C.

These people, we find, claim an identity and uniqueness explicable only because of the strange beauty revealed in that original vision of the Castle. They had an outlook which was at total variance with the peoples, the cultures, and the religions surrounding them in the contemporary Middle East. Set in the middle of worshipers of Ra, Marduk, Ibis, Amon, Gilgamesh, Hadad, Nannar, Dagon, Ea, Baal, Moloch, Astarte, and scores of other gods and goddesses, the Jews stand out almost eerily.

The fundamental trait of their outlook was a firm persuasion: from beyond the height of the skies, beyond the point where all human efforts stop and fail, a power had come, choosing the Jews to be witnesses of a truth, and, in so doing, touching that portion of the earth where they, Jews, lived, and thus making it specially separate—"holy," in that sense.

In their imagery of the Castle, that which was "in the highest," that which was immeasurably distant from the human condition, had come within measurable distance of the Jew and his land, focusing at one historic place: Jerusalem. And it had so happened as much from the choice made by the Invisible and the Eternal as through the acceptance by the Jew, through his faith. By believing in his chosenness, he had scaled the impossible height that forever yawned between visible and invisible, eternal and mortal; scaled it, so that in him, in his sacred land, in his people, that height of heaven on earth became the hallmark of his Castle vision. Heaven had touched Earth at Jerusalem.

Here we are talking of an *experience*, not of a concept nor of a doctrine. It was the experience of belonging to a group which would never have to cease. They would transcend all historical barriers—those events in human time which normally spell the cessation of so many groups of human beings, because they were promised perpetuity on this land. By that token they would testify to the transcendence of human existence. For all the world, it was as if the permanency ascribed by believers to their god and to the divine was transferred holus-bolus to a people as a people. They were to be a physical expression of that divine being in human terms, from generation to generation. And thus in their Castle vision Jews saw themselves as witnesses to the basic fact that man and his earth were saved, are continuously saved, from the one thing man fears: the insignificance of death, nothingness, oblivion. Within that core lies the strange beauty of the Jewish vision: The ongoingness of this people in the House of Elohim and at the Gate of the Skies, Jerusalem.

The beauty of that vision did not lie principally in physical form. It enhanced the mountains and plains of that land with poetry—but not merely esthetically, as Homer and Sophocles did for Greece. It inspired nothing like the novels we find in pharaonic Egypt; but it limned stories of human hope and perfidy, of divine compassion and mortal greatness. It produced no Plato or Aristotle in philosophy, no giant like Ptolemy in geography, no Erastothenes or Archimedes in mathematics. But it gave birth to a way of life enshrining the sonship and brotherhood of all men. Compared to the beauty of Greece and to the glory of Rome, it sometimes appeared stark, comfortless, unrelieved by the golden hues of a humanism, and unrelentingly bereft of that decoration and decadence which always appear as inseparable wife and daughter of human culture. It was an exclusionary Christian civilization, not some innate inability in Jews, which prevented in early times the flowering of a Jewish humanism. Later, when Moses Mendelssohn made the breakthrough, the Jewish genius flowed through all the arts and sciences of the West. But the beauty of the vision was not thus achieved.

For that beauty was not one of simple logic or of pure reason. It was rather the beauty of an englobing intuition: that there is at the back of human lives an abyss of light more blinding and unfathomable than any abyss of darkness which human misery can discover. It is the abyss of existence; the fact that all things truly are, and that man himself is incredibly, and sometimes almost incredulously, real; the fundamental fact of being, as against not being. It is unthinkable, yet we cannot unthink it, though we may sometimes be unthinking and especially unthanking about it. And the intuition tells more: that this reality does outweigh, literally to infinity, all lesser regrets or arguments for negation and despair. That under all man's pains, and throughout all the sufferings of belief, there is a subconscious substance of gratitude: gratitude for God's fatherhood, for man's sonship, for the earth's blessing by the divine, and for the Jews' assignment by God to bear perpetual witness to the humanness of man's existence. For this in the Jewish vision is the salvation of the world and of all in it.

When we examine the history of Jews between the death of Saul (1000 B.C.) and the year 135 A.D., we can see the human fabric in which the Jews came to clothe their early vision of the Castle. They adopted ideas: covenant, kingship, priesthood, temple, shrine, bible, midrash. They took on an entire mythology to explain the origin of mankind and the universe, and an "official history" of their own ethnic origins, together with a minutely detailed code of moral behavior. Later still, they adopted Greek ideas of immortality, the nature of divinity, rules of logic; and Iranian ideas on a resurrection from the dead, a last day for the world, salvation, and a messianic figure. This process culminated in the Second Commonwealth. Between 150 and 100 B.C. the Jews, starting as a small group huddled around their sacred mountain, Jerusalem, defeated one of the great monarchies of the Middle East, expanded their territories from the Mediterranean to the Arabian desert and from Egypt to Damascus, overcame vast areas to the east, proselytized vast populations, and carried on vigorous conversionist propaganda in imperial Rome. In the last twenty years before Jesus, the temple was rebuilt on the spot where Abraham received the Promise. Here was Temple again as symbol of Jewish permanence. In this Place.

By 135 A.D., all this was obliterated: the Roman monolith made sure of that. A vibrant Christianity and, later, an all-conquering Islam—both appropriating Jerusalem, the Bible, and the immemorial heritage—finished the grim job. Rabbi Akiva and the Men of Yavneh created the "fence of the Law," an ad hoc defense against encroachment. A whole new way of life was developed in the Jewish Diaspora, within the iron hegemonies of Christians and Muslims, as the only means to ensure still the permanence of an identifiable people.

The Jewish spirit and its vision lived and survived, snatching its life and, with that, its integrity out of the jaws of death. Silenced, it sank easily through deeps under deeps of darkness and complex concepts; until it lay like a stone at the farthest bottom of life, no longer aware, yet alive with a peculiar lucidity and coherence; like a minute and fiercely burning particle of being that knew itself as a chosen thing, composed entirely of the stubborn will to live. "Trust me," its hard unwinking eye of life said. "Trust me. I stay forever."

Probably it could have so stayed for many further centuries if Hitlerian Germany had not attempted to obliterate all traces of the Jews from Earth. No psychological technique known to us and no method of historical analysis currently in vogue can assess the effect produced in the Jewish spirit by Adolf Hitler's planned and executed liquidation of six million Jews during World War II. It has been described as attempted genocide. That, indeed, it was. But this does not tell us what the Jewish spirit underwent: a sudden shock of understanding that no continuation in normative Judaism beyond the first third of the twentieth century could preserve the Jewish vision. It was not enough. The combined powers of Torah, Talmud, traditions, customs, and laws were no longer supremely valent. No more. This was the lesson.

To repose essential hopes in the tensile fabric of normative Judaism, its expectations of final resurrection and of ultimate security, this no longer guaranteed Jewish perseverance in existence. No further. Even to proceed along the leisurely lines of the Herzlian Return would not suffice. A human storm unleashed with sufficient fury could undo all such hopes and make all these expectations illusory.

Beyond the powerful devastation of the Jewish spirit administered by the Hitlerian terror in unspeakable doses of shame, agony, and death, there arose a still more powerful imperative: Get back! Go up to the Land! All of you! Go up to Jerusalem! Reach for the ancient vision! Through all the veils of unknowing. Through each layer imposed by thirty centuries of Jewish existence on the periphery of alien human societies.

At that moment, the taut dialectic at the heart of Jewish existence bedeviled the Jew. It strung him out in tension between two awesome alternatives. As in any real dialectic, the negative pole was the heart of darkness in him: the possibility of annihilation in some form or other; the possibility that by virtue of any given circumstance or change he initiated, he would cease to be a Jewish man: be less than the man he was, or other than the man he planned to be. The positive pole was his eternal vision, the ever-present abyss of existence. And from the beginning of the new tension, there was no real choice. It was: "Next year in Jerusalem!" It was: "Hang on to Jerusalem with your teeth!" It was: "Attack and attack and attack!" It was: "Good night and goodbye from Jerusalem." And, finally, it was Moshe Dayan: "We have returned to this most sacred shrine, never to part from it again."

When you turn to the present, then, and walk through the streets of Jerusalem, history peers from every corner, and cliché dates keep rising to the surface of your memory. From 638 A.D. until 1948, this was a predominantly Muslim city and its land almost exclusively Muslim.

From 1948 to June 1967, it was a divided city: Jews held one part, the New City; the Muslims held the Old City. For those nineteen years, the New City was like a cluster of grapes clinging to three sides of a solid, walled, resistant core: the Old City where, Muslims hold, the Prophet ascended to Heaven and where, Christians believe, Jesus was crucified, buried, and rose again from the dead. Now something new has taken over. "We have liberated Jerusalem," intoned Moshe Dayan on June 7, 1967, as he stood before the Old City, "we have reunified the torn City, the capital of Israel."

Today, the city is all one, under Israeli rule. You can now walk unimpeded by barbed wire, armed men, and hateful opposition, from Talpiot in the south of the city through the Old City and on northward to Ramallah. Or starting at the Dome of the Rock in the Old City, with the Dead Sea at your back, out through the Jaffa Gate, along Jaffa Road westward through the New City to the edges of the highway leading to Tel Aviv. New apartment houses, low-cost housing, government ministries, institutes, shops, offices are being erected through and around the Old City. Streets are being widened. The aged dividing walls are coming down. City engineers are organizing plumbing and sanitation. Archeologists are digging areas untouched for over 1500 years. On the City outskirts, very old towns like Emmaus, Beit, Nuba Yalu have been completely eradicated; landscaping, eucalyptus groves, and new settlements cover their sites. An estimated 900,000 Israeli settlers are expected to immigrate to the City. The Old City is ringed already with Jewish settlements. The clinging grapes have at last poured their juice into an old core. Through its historic gates—Dung Gate, Jaffa Gate, Herod's Gate, Zion Gate, New Gate, St. Stephen's Gate—its narrow terraced streets, its arched alleyways, another life is racing into the antique arteries of the City. It will never be the same again. The old will cease to exist soon. There will soon be one homogeneous City quickened by the new vision of the Castle. That vision, however, is elusive. We, today, like Samson once in Gaza, are eyeless. But we can feel and reach for its contours while we beware of the ghosts.

Back at the Wall, within a few days of June 6 the homes of 129 Muslim families are razed, their 1000 members dismissed. An esplanade is created in front of the Wall. A row of Israeli flags flutters at the edge of the new space. And as you take a leisurely walk across, from the flags toward the Wall, two shadowy figures walk hand-in-hand, silently, doggedly by your side, each claiming attention, announcing its name and its message, and formulating its version of the Castle. Both are essential contributors to the vision.

One impressively styles itself Hard Facts and presents its message as realism. It will have you visit this scene as the now peaceful monument to a military victory: this Wall, it insists, together with the state of Israel, has been carved by steel and fire from the heart of a 1300-year-old Muslim homeland; and the twisted lips of the resulting wound are black with suffering. Only in this way was a return possible to Jerusalem. And, therefore, only thus

can the new vision be achieved. Momentarily, concentrated vigilance is required. But this will change. For the
suffering will be immemorialized; it will cease. The passion to survive will give way, duly, to the compassion of
man's brotherhood with man. All panic and the near hysteria of threatened extinction will fade. In its place: the
strength of peace and forgiveness for those who made Jews
fight them in order that Judaism survive.

Another figure with yarmulke, peot curls, the ketub-
bah and the keter Torah, the seven-branched candlestick
and the prayer-shawl presents its message as the Hope
confirmed. This scene, it states gently but firmly, is what
Rabbi Akiva and the Men of Yavneh made possible. And
so many others: the patient men who copied Talmud and
Midrashim all those centuries, the jurists, theologians,
teachers, rabbis, the Sabbath assemblies moaning and
swaying in supplication, all those who guarded the Covenant. Hitherto, this gentleness has been defensive and this
strength was only patience and an iron-souled determination to hold on even when there was nothing left to hold
on to. But now a fresh note has entered: the Hope of a future has been confirmed as joy in the present. This Wall,
originally a memorial to love remembered, is now a memorial to love itself. And as you turn away from it to stroll
through the Old and the New Cities, hints of the millennial
beauty begin to appear.

Jerusalem is rapidly becoming totally new. In seeking
there the new vision of the Castle, you first notice what
does not belong essentially to that vision. Manifestly, the
state of Israel is not a professedly religious one. And in
this light, you judge the bedlam of believers and beliefs in
modern Jerusalem. You do not see Jerusalem as the city of
three religions: Muslims—visible, audible, holding as best
they can to their shrines; Christians—Greek Orthodox,
Russian Orthodox, Syrians, Melchites, Roman Catholics,

Armenians, Copts, Protestants of a dozen denominations; Jews—Orthodox, Conservative, Reform, Jews for Jesus, Christians for Moses, Neturei Karta, Bahai. Nor must you see Jerusalem as a city of rabbis, ministers, muezzins, priests, archimandrites, bishops, patriarchs, monks, nuns. Nor Jerusalem as a city of contrasts and extremes: Mea Shearim peopled with dark-robed, bearded, hatted, solemn-faced men, side by side with residential suburbs like Beit Ha-Kerem; the Hebrew University campus—a gleaming display of new architecture, modern glass, chrome, cement, and steel, within a stone's throw of 800-year-old buildings; the old fortress of David shoulder-to-shoulder with the Benedictine Monastery of the Virgin's Dormition; the Shrine of the Book, the Shrine of the Prophet, the Shrine of Jesus within the same city limits; and sabras who visit the Via Dolorosa where Jesus walked whipped, bleeding, and stumbling to his crucifixion, asking in puzzlement: "But why didn't he hit back?"

None of all this appears now to you as the vehicle of the new vision. It will not reveal the Jewish face of beauty. The Islam of Muslims and the Christianity of Christians are destined to be ranged in the historical show-cases of Jerusalem. They are already of the past. But, more deeply, the strong face of Israeli Jewishness and the gentle persevering face of traditional Judaism are everywhere in Jerusalem with you; instinctively you feel the pervading realization that both of these will cede to the new. One has waxed strong because it was the only way to get back to the place where once the vision had been experienced. That vision was always tied to this city. For over 1800 years, Jews were not physically in possession of the place. Others have been. Getting back there, therefore, involved a forceful taking over and a refashioning of the land. The other had evolved because it was the only means of survival. Now the achievement of land and city has meant the end of patient survival and defensive piety. For the first time since the time of Saul, and as in the time of Saul almost 3000 years ago—there is no longer any felt need for temple, priesthood, coded ethical laws of personal integrity, or the fence of legal prescription.

The Jew of Israel is reaching back, not as it were to discover and recapture the face of beauty once shown to his ancestors and since veiled. That wide and long procession of reachers began with Abraham and, on June 6, 1967, was concentrated at a small length of the wall. In a few battle-weary soldiers with the guns of Jordanian resistance still thundering in their ears, it has reached and is reaching merely to complete the chain of mystic communication and transmission.

With repossession of the City, the flow of Jewish initiative took on once again a verve and thrust for the Castle which it has not known since the time that David and his men overcame the Philistines. That thrust is, of course, both a desired thing and a risk-laden gamble. The Israeli undertakes it solely on the basis of his hope in history and a belief in his chosenness on this land. It takes place within a modern sociopolitical structure which has nothing of a theocracy about it. As far as the eye sees, it has everything possible of the technological efficiency, the scientific excellence, the mechanization of daily life, the military prowess and primacy, and the go-getting changefulness of the West and, particularly, of the United States. We in the West have paid a very costly price for our achievements: we are beset apparently by a rampant materialism which threatens to throttle our life. In the overarching ceiling of their national consciousness and ever-watchful security and within the impressive enclosure of Israel, the Israelis claim indubitably: we will create a completely modern ambience for our Jewishness, as a frame and setting for that beauty made accessible to us centuries ago when Heaven touched Earth here.

With success, and when the ancient beauty shines again in the Land and in the City, Jews all over the world will have to answer anew the long-debated question: What is Jewishness? And all other men will question themselves about their own identity. All of us have need of that beauty.

4

CONSTANTINOPLE
Light and Life of Men

If you live for some time on friendly terms with the inhabitants of the Sirkeci quarter in Istanbul, you will hear in their story telling some odd references to a phantom horseman—Kira, they call him—to be seen any night in May and November of each year. Tall, bearded, helmeted, armed, never bothering with mortal onlookers, staring sightlessly ahead, he gallops soundlessly, as phantoms do, over houses, minarets, streets, from north to south, stopping and dismounting at the Topkapi Sarayi museum. There he lays his shield on the ground, takes the bit from his horse's mouth and kisses it. At that moment, a broad river of brightness falls from the night skies onto his shield. For some instants, they tell you, the darkened huddled masses of the city become transparent: gaily colored streams of light well up in silence from beneath the streets as if modern Istanbul had never been anything else but a transparent cloak thrown over an ever-burning incandescence. In a flash, it is all over: *"Kira gider,"* your informant concludes. Kira goes. He is Kira Bizansli, Kira the Byzantine. Darkness returns. Istanbul, city of Sultans, lying on the Bosporus like an anciently ravaged but still beautiful whore, sleeps on.

Over sixteen hundred years ago—to be precise, on September 19, 324 A.D., a bearded, helmeted horseman at the head of some 110,000 foot soldiers and 7000 cavalry dismounted at the spot now occupied by the Topkapi but then a clearing on the outskirts of a small city, Byzantion, already a thousand years old. He laid his shield on the ground, kissed the bit from his horse's mouth, and gazed up at the sky. It was Friday. His full name: Flavius Valerius Constantinus. Known in history books as Constantine the Great. On his shield: two Greek letters, X (chi) and P (rho)—the first two letters in the name of Christ. The chi-rho monogram, as it was called later; now latent in Turkish folklore as Kira. His horse's bit: the nail driven through the hand of Jesus pinning it to his cross.

Yesterday, Thursday, Constantine fought and won a ferocious battle two miles from here; now all his known world belongs to him alone. Twelve years previously, the cross of Jesus appeared to him superimposed on the noonday sun; in that sign, he had won the battle of the Milvian Bridge and the Roman Empire. Today, it is his second vision. The final one. "I am the apostle of the Highest Divinity," he declared. "All the light of Paradise, Wisdom, is now in this world. Is its life. Its peace. Here. With its own. The All-Powerful: he who is absolutely masterful, the Pantokrator, has become man. We have become divine, according to his promise. We shall receive him in his own city. On this spot. The city of me, Constantine, *Konstantinou polis,* will house his light, solidly, forever."

Six weeks later, on November 11, Constantine traced the plans of his city with a spear point. Its site was a pear-shaped promontory washed on the north by a four-and-one-half-mile inlet called the Golden Horn, on the east by the Bosporus, on the south by the Sea of Marmora. Five years and six months later, on May 11, 330, the finished city was solemnly consecrated as the House of Christ's light. Sitting on seven hills, as Rome, Stuttgart, and San Francisco do, its walls ran for five miles and enclosed a magnificent forum (where Constantine's statue stood on a hundred-foot column of red porphyry with a twenty-foot marble base), senate house, imperial palace, hippodrome, acropolis, the Bukoleon harbor, the Augustaion Square, streets, porticoes, houses, shops, statuary, water cisterns, sewers, baths, and three main churches: Agia Irene (dedicated to peace); the Holy Apostles (where Constantine would be buried in the summer of 337); and Agia Sophia (dedicated to Holy Wisdom, rebuilt by his son, perfected two centuries later by the emperor Justinian). By Constantine's death, its population was nearly 100,000. Six centuries later, its walls ran for fourteen miles, enclosing thirteen towns; its population was slightly more than a million; its annual income was the equivalent of one and one-half million gold dollars, and nothing so magnificent had ever existed in the world of men. Thus Constantinople began.

But, as Ernest Renan remarked over eighty years ago, "It was not merely a city which thus began to exist. It was a condition, a human state of the environment. And the whole of Western culture was changed by its presence." Constantine did not tell his official biographer, Eusebius, the details of his vision on that Friday. He did say enough for us to know its essence: the source and the possessor of all power had entered the human condition, the universe of men. There was now present among men and women that which exclusively gave them reality and meaning as men and women. This was Jesus, the Pantokrator. With him he brought and installed Heaven on Earth—now centered here at Constantinople.

Central to that Constantinople vision was the one trait of Jesus that has always fascinated men, even those who did or do not believe in him: the calm assumption of total authority which he wore quietly and as a matter of course; his absolute mastery, his supreme control. In human annals, he is the only one, we are told, who passed through a human span with patent confidence, unquestioning ease, complete grip over the men and the women, the events, and the elements which composed the texture of his life; drawing life from death, promising life against death, never at a loss, never beset by an ultimate he did not seem to know beforehand and to encompass with a greater power. He appears as the epitome of what all men lacked and would always lack, however powerful they became, however uniquely they stood out: power over all, perpetually. The absolutely masterful. The Pantokrator. The perpetual model of human greatness. The ideal of men's yearnings. The refuge for their weakness. And this is a basic trait all have recognized in Jesus of Nazareth.

What stamped this vision at Constantinople with a special hallmark forever was the insertion of this Jesus into the Greek ideal as a source of new life for it. And, to express this revivified ideal, they invented a special technique and a special life style—the Byzantine style. When all is said and done, that ideal was one of human beauty, flawless, perpetually fresh and young, without pain, and—above all—dwelling in light. Light for the Greeks was the sap of life, the ambient of wisdom, had a sacred and divine quality, was the reward of heroes and the perpetual possession of the divine. It made the human day possible. It showed off all glory, human and divine. It was the opposite of night and of night's first cousin, death. It was the sheen of beauty and the luster of eyes. Light was life, was wisdom, was peace. Within the tranquillity of eternity's smile and vibrancy revealed in Jesus, all the preceding glory and beauty and light of the Hellenic world was gathered up, rid of its mortalness, and embellished anew.

The plastic technique used to convey that vision now appears to us moderns as a humbling secret of those dead ancients: an alchemy unknown and undiscoverable, some mysterious skill in the use of materials all available to us today: glass, stone, paint, oil, gold, silver, precious stones. But their secret lay in a technique they developed of making all these dead and lifeless materials move, come to life, flow, detach themselves from wall fixture and ceiling and pillar. By means of sunlight, refraction, candle flame, oil lamps, they achieved in the vertical and the pendent the same sense of movement which we perceive in the horizontal when we watch the winking, waving, and changing of pebbles at the bottom because of the transparent waters of a stream. They contrasted the differing gleams of marble and granite, paired off the welling of light in curves with the ricochet of shadows on angles, joined recessive and dominant colors in mutual comparison. No object in this world was excluded from their draftsmanship: fruit, trees, stones, oceans, plants, birds, animals, humans, waters, mountains, houses. All, in fact, had to be used because the Pantokrator had resurrected all in a new earth and a new heaven. All was now new and newly glorious.

Thereby the former Hellenic calm attained by the Greeks was quickened into a romantic excitement. That still and beautiful light which Greeks had captured was translated into the soundless reverberations of clashing shadows and flames. The hammered fragments, hard and motionless, of the mosaics cemented centuries ago into the walls still move today. They become for your eyes fluid, volatile, traveling in different directions with the movement of your eyes, the shift of your head, the wave of a candle flame. All becomes movement within the lightsomeness of midnight blue flecked by warm earth colors—black, white, brown, purple, indigo, green, yellow.

The historical record little examined and much distorted by Christians in the West, woefully misinterpreted by the generation of men who made the European Renaissance 1400 years later, tells a fascinating story of how this came about. An explosion in the human spirit took place in Jerusalem and Palestine between the death of Jesus (approximately 29 A.D.) and the destruction of Jerusalem in 135 A.D. But the purest line of development created by that explosion did not travel westward to Rome and still farther westward to Western Europe. It spread up through those areas we now call Syria, Lebanon, Armenia, and Turkey, across the Bosporus, into northern Greece, and down to the Aegean and all the islands. The first creation of the new faith was not a Latin church feeding on the dead works and mortal necessity of a decadent Roman civilization. It was, for all the world, as if the light and beauty and symmetry and life so pathetically and wanly described by the Greeks as delicious fruits forbidden to mere mortals suddenly became the inheritance of mortals. One man, Constantine, was great enough to see what no Latin or Roman ever saw: that, indeed, a totally new order had come, but that it consecrated—not negated—all that Greece had achieved.

Constantine was born in what is now Yugoslavia. His mother, Helena, daughter of an innkeeper, and his father, Constantius, a man of very obscure origins, were Asiatic Greeks of mixed Greek, Celtic, Latin, Scythian, and Asiatic blood. Constantine, nicknamed "Bull neck" by his soldiers, was tall, muscular, bullet headed, loose limbed, heavy lidded, prognathous, rather unlovely in face, an excellent horseman and redoubtable hand-to-hand fighter, ruthless, multilingual (Greek, Latin, Pict, Gaulish, at least two Germanic dialects, Persian), widely traveled (all over Europe, parts of Near Asia and North Africa), acutely intelligent, cunning, self-righteous, messianic. He assassinated, tortured, liquidated, plotted, destroyed, laid waste, repented, preached, reasoned, legislated, built, designed, chaired international meetings, caroused, lechered, swore, drank deeply, hunted, loved, fathered children, pitied, protected, taught, governed, and latterly decided practically on his deathbed to be baptized in the name of that Jesus in whom he had already believed for over a quarter of a century. But his lasting achievement was to make it possible for the glory of Greece to be perpetuated in a fresh form. This was his Constantinople.

Due to his decision, what we find about three centuries later belongs to the order of all that is fabulous, "all that men and women never seem deserving of," to use a phrase of Gertrude Stein. Renan was correct. We find a new human environment, not merely in the city of Constantinople, but throughout a large area of the then known world: present Greece, Yugoslavia, and Albania; parts of Egypt, Italy, Bulgaria, Rumania, and the Soviet Union; most of present Turkey and Palestine. You could take a map of Europe and the Near East for that time and sketch on it mystically, as on an ikon, a strange and wonder-making light, intense at Constantinople, reaching out in lambent tongues over the area of the Byzantine empire, dimming at the eastern edges of Spain, France, the southern and western borders of Germanic and Slavic lands, and at the Italian Alps; fading into the jungles, sands, and obscurity of Africa and Asia. This is Constantinople. Greater Constantinople. For Constantinople—or Byzance, as it is so often called—was not merely a city. It was a style of humanness spread over a definite area.

To understand that humanness—without it, there can be no ascension of the spirit for us to the vision of Constantinople—we in the West must leap over a difficult barrier, like jumping out of our cultural skins. What happened at that early time was in the nature of strict continuity: the human ideal of the Greeks was assumed and perfected by what was more than human, thereby becoming more humanly perfect, more humanly beautiful. But we are ignorant of this continuity. As heirs of the humanism and science-oriented tradition of Western Europe since 1400, we have been inured to a domino view of ancient and modern history. Automatically we think within that time frame: first, the Greeks who tried to think rationally and who caught in plastic arts the beauty and symmetry of human reality—and they fell; then, the Romans who put all in order, gave us law—and they fell; then, the Christians who throttled Greek rationalism, banned the beauty, borrowed Roman order as a new imperialism, subjugated the Western mind for over 1200 years—and they fell; then the humanists who revived the Greek ideal at the Renaissance—and they fell; then, the men who took to objective research and scientific knowledge—and, lately, they are falling and failing. We now, it is said, we are failing likewise. Our turn for the ax.

The human scene is thus taken as an inglorious jungle, empty of mercy, thriving on death, the kitchen midden of cannibal growths: all things dying each other's life, living on the other's death, each inevitably reduced merely to a featureless clay and dust which the succeeding generation runs through its fingers as it, too, faces an identical and certain fate. But the historical facts tell us otherwise: that the Greek ideal did not thus die, was not shrouded in darkness, when belief in Jesus seized the Greek world of the fourth to sixth centuries. Rather, having previously peaked and attained a maximum, it had been frozen into a helpless fixity, an immobility, until in those centuries and within that belief seizure, it was once more liquified and further refined, thus being prolonged in visible existence until the late fifteenth century when Asiatic Turks took Constantinople and that ideal, as part of the vision, fled to the mountains overhead and hid its face in the crowding stars.

Our grasp of all this has been muddied over with erroneous statements which must be eschewed. The Greek ideal had many borrowings often ascribed to Greek authorship: mathematics from India, symmetry from the Persians, a sense of beauty from the Asiatics, dialectical argument from the Iranians, science from the Ionians, music from the Lydians, meters from the Carians, law from the Semites, alphabet from the Arabians, the institution of mystery from the Egyptians.

When you shred away all derivatives and accretions from the Greek ideal, you are left with its one originality: a persuasion that a human being had an innate dignity as human, some inner condition of the human self, which made any human being capable of total perfection, total happiness, total beauty, total truth—whether he achieved it or not. That innate dignity they conveyed through the image of what was most precious and peculiarly endowed in their geographical area: light. That and all else they acquired was used to explain, express, depict, and celebrate that dignity of man. After centuries of its cultivation and pursuit in art and politics and war, inevitably they saw it as frustrated—no matter how symmetrically they arranged the parts of their humanness, no matter what supernal tranquillity they infused into that symmetry.

The home of that ideal was not merely the Greece "discovered" by the humanists of the Renaissance, sung by the romantic poets of the eighteenth century, visited today by a yearly two million tourists. That is merely a rocky delta in the Mediterranean. But the Greek ideal's home ran from the Ganges to Sicily and from the Red Sea to the Caspian. At its height, the temple and the statue and the agora and the democratic assembly and the mosaic and the column and the frieze and the poetry—all the articulations of the ideal, were frozen in the fixity of a *ne plus ultra* nobody ever pronounced but everyone felt: it was as far as human endeavor of itself could go, indeed ever did go.

The explosive belief in Jesus was revivification of dead forms and precious liquid to melt that fixity. The statue by that time represented man as having nothing more to achieve, physically now finished and complacent and premonitory of decay; with world-considering eyes gazing at nothing, veiled and half-veiled, weary and wary of world and vision alike; bodies as conventional as commas and periods in correct prose. Suddenly a fabulous movement and life seizes all: the limbs move; the Byzantine eyes of drilled ivory gaze upward on a vision. The Parthenon frieze had riders stock still in movement, caught in a moment of cruel time. In Sant'Apollinare Nuovo at Ravenna, on three banks of mosaics, the procession of white-robed men and women move across flowering fields with the Magi to greet the Virgin and the Child, within the fluid eternity of light and color. The Greek temple is transformed and turned inside out: columns as well as paintings are put inside; the light—always excluded—now is shed inside. The Greek theater, always a scene of man's innate dignity and of his fatal flaw, now becomes the stage for a new rite: all the ancient color and gesture and music and cantillation and language are transmitted and transformed in the rain-colored vestments, the silver music, the symbolic acts, the Greek prayers, the swelling intervals of silence and song, the commentary of the chorus—now the

choir. All was adapted to sing of, and to represent sceni-
cally and theatrically man's innate dignity now become
divine because Jesus had become human and God's all
power could prevent man from being trapped by the fatal
flaw or damned to nothingness by the hubris which pursued every Greek hero and heroine. Indeed, a successful
hero was now possible, because the Hero par excellence
had come: sage and athlete, eternal and human, in one
person. The central Eleusinian mysteries of the ancient
land became the mysteries celebrating one mother and one
son who no longer died each year.

But the humanness thus achieved involved much more.
All daily and public life was affected. The ancient life of
the ancient agora, meeting place for litigants, merchants,
politicians, lovers, housewives, was transferred to the
church where the newly shed light and shadow and color
gave substance to arguments, voting, discussions, cabal-
lings, love trysts, and popular celebrations. The dying dialectic of philosophers took up the fresh life of the new
word, and the intricacies of God, man, trinity, and truth
now made available; barbers and carpenters, we are told,
expounded theology; women claimed equal rights because
of Mary; drovers swore with theological terms; artisans
debated angelology. Symbols changed hands and were refurbished: Apollo's laurels became the Virgin's; the pea-
cock became the symbol of eternal life and knowing. Byzance, in the words of a ninth-century visitor, was a whole
population in motion and pursuit of discussion and feeling
thought. "If you ask someone for change," wrote Gregory
of Nyssa, "he philosophizes about the Begotten and the
Unbegotten." Religion, esthetics, music, practical life
were all one. The vision made building, picture, pattern,
people, city, road, sea, land, and country seem but one
single image. Constantinople became the city par excellence. Men referred to it simply as "the City." *Stin*

polin. And even when the Turks took it in 1453, they did not name it; they converted the two Greek words into Stimboli which later became the modern Istanbul.

A lot has been made out of the supposed antirational and antiscience character of Constantinople. But this is fatuous. The fact is that at least two hundred years before Constantinople was founded, the scientific urge of the Greeks had stopped in its tracks. Some vital interest in science had run out of men's lives; they were more concerned with survival and more tortured by a radical question such as: What does it mean to be human? than by an inductive problem such as: Is the world flat or round? When learning, culture, cuisine, clothes, civic behavior, public justice, and international relations were reaching their lowest ebb and the Emperor of the West, Charlemagne, could not read and wore the same shirt for over twenty-two years, all those aspects of life were flourishing at Constantinople with a decor never before known.

There was no love lost between East and West. Rome, which dominated the West, saw in Constantinople its arch rival. Westerners in general saw Byzance as fair booty. What they did not know and understand about the trailing one-thousand-year glory of Byzance was covered with an obloquy and ignorance that persists until today: the history of Constantinople "is nothing but a tissue of revolts, seditions, and perfidies," wrote Montesquieu. "A tedious and uniform tale of weakness and misery," Gibbon pontificated. "A monstrous story of intrigues; of priests, eunuchs, and women; of poisonings, of conspiracies, of uniform ingratitude, of perpetual fratricide," commented Lecky.

Toward the end of the Middle Ages, perhaps the greatest experiment in the total living of the Castle vision at Constantinople was failing. Its empire was reduced in size, beset by internal struggles, betrayed and attacked by

Western European powers. The original exaltation in the vision had become diluted into a fierce pride and a contempt for all outsiders. The Orthodox Church headed by the Patriarch of Constantinople had become the jealous guardian of the truth—and it now had several price tags. Transmission of values became a freezing of effort. Learning did not change and grow; it ossified. The beauty of the vision became identified with the various nationalisms involved: "Sacred land of Greece," "Holy Mother Russia." For Serbs, Slovenes, Rumanians, Cypriots, Alexandrians, Armenians, their ethnic identity coincided with their religion and their political bias was colored by both.

By the beginning of the fifteenth century, it was clear that no European power intended Constantinople to continue in existence. Already, much of the Greek mainland was occupied by Latins, Franks, Venetians, Genoese, Germans. Their hatred for Byzance was so great and so known to the Byzantines that, on the eve of Constantinople's fall to the Turks, its last great minister of state, Lukas Notaras, stated pithily: "Better the Sultan's turban than the Cardinal's hat"—a reference to the constant eroding of Byzance by Rome. Sultan Mehmet II, nicknamed "The Gentleman," moved in on the doomed city with army and navy on April 2, 1453. It was just spring: the storks were building their nests in the rooftops; orchards were bursting into flower; the nightingales had returned from the south and sang in the woods. On Tuesday, May 29, 1453, at 1:30 A.M., the final assault began. In the afternoon, the city fell. Two days later, Mehmet mounted the altar slab in Agia Sophia and made a solemn profession of his Islam. It was over. The Castle vision had lost its visible and human house.

It took refuge in the long exile of Eastern Orthodoxy. Yet so bright had that vision shone and so completing was its beauty that in the lands where it once reigned, there still persists its lingering memory and an as yet uneroded attachment to its heritage. What a Russian chronicler wrote in the late tenth century is still true today: "We cannot forget that beauty."

It was a beauty achieved by a personal outlook, a public life, and a sociopolitical system, which—all three— arose from a unitary belief and from that human tranquillity only possible when the most agonizing questions have been answered by unimpeachable authority and universally accepted solutions. The Castle is not only envisioned; it is instilled and lived. The basic religious belief that animated all in Constantinople and Byzance was utterly different in quality from the Roman and Western version that emerged in Europe around the eleventh century. In the latter, God was a shapely structure of describable struts called predicamental relations; Jesus was a Westerner, thought in Latin, and ruled with a scepter; salvation came by a rubber-stamp parchment; man was a human animal, half-holy, half-vicious; to divide the world between Portugal and Spain with the stroke of a pen, as Pope Clement did in 1545, was more Christlike than loving your enemies; Satan (never the dignified fallen archangel of Byzance) was a horned scarecrow—you laughed at him when you weren't running scared, or you identified him with the local rabbi and cut his throat on Good Friday; belief was defined by mental clarity; heaven was a carrot held at a distance—you trotted in tune to reach it.

That is why the faith of Byzance is now strange and alien to us. At the end of our culture, and beset by ominous fissures in the world we once presumed to be unassailable, we labor under a double disadvantage, as we now walk through Constantinople and examine the fragments of those men's vision-telling monuments. We start with fragments, not with the vision that fathered the now fragmented monuments. And human reality now has been reduced to what is measurable by its duration, its location in space, and its chemical properties—something exclusive of the invisible, the impalpable, the ineffable. Otherwise, we cry panic: "We are at the mercy of the irrational!" For us as Christians, as scientists, as moderns, the Byzantines had a knowledge we today deny to be possible. Even when we try to grasp it, the try is in vain: we seek a concept of what is nonconceptual, what is neither prelogical nor postlogical, neither prerational nor postrational, neither arational nor irrational, neither conscious nor subconscious, nor unconscious. But these are the only categories now remaining to us.

That faith was the purest expression of the original belief that followed on the death of Jesus of Nazareth. As a gospel, it had nothing of the strident prophetism of Matthew, of the factual reportage of Mark, or of the intellectual research of Luke. It was a warming, loving gospel first formulated by John and coming to us in Greek: "In the beginning was the Word. . . . In him was life. . . . That life was the light for men, the true light which enlightens any man born into this universe. . . . And he lived with us and we saw his glory. . . ." Where the ancient Greek greeted beauty, throwing a silken veil over it because, being its own sanctification, it had already receded into the mysteries of the world, the Byzantines held all in this world to be sanctified from without and therefore to dwell in the "*lux increatus*" of the divine. It is of this that you become dimly aware—without concepts or words to match it—when you examine Byzantine monuments.

Among these many visible fragments as among flint stones for striking a fire, you can perceive the whole vision of Constantinople. You find that those who worked there acquired a superb art: life and movement, not depicted as such for your perception of them, but so conveyed to you that, while perceiving them, you live and move with them. It takes a while, but you eventually know that what you are living through them is the life of the ancient vision, that the movement which integrates you is the flowing interchange between the eternal which has come to rest here and the mortal which has been immortalized by its coming.

This happens to you, for instance, when you enter Agia Sophia in Istanbul today through one of the nine doors in the vestibule. It is a domed basilica with immense pendentives, extended by two systems of hemicycles, flanked by lateral galleries and aisles which, in turn, are vaulted by minor domes. Fling a note of music upward. And it travels undulatingly with a life all its own through dome within dome, from hemicycle to arcade, and beyond through unseen corridors and passages high up behind the facades to still further corners, unexpectedly issuing again in solemn arpeggios, speaking to you as a return message from behind and above and each side. Standing in the south gallery, you find that you are listening not merely to beautiful acoustics. Some voice is speaking inside you; and the syllables are translated simultaneously into the movement of the color, shade, and light above your head. The walls are singing with moving light and you are slowly being warmed by some holy fire.

You notice then that the walls and domes around are veiled in what appear to be gigantic tapestries let down from Heaven and whose measurable dimensions now seem to partake of the immensity of all space glittering in the movement of gold, white, and red stars advancing to full brightness and retreating to a glow. The hands of John the Baptist move in entreaty. The lips of the Virgin and her eyes move in prayer. Jesus, Pantokrator, youthful, calm, radiant with divinity, almost with a dreamy ease of total power and beauty, moves his right hand in blessing. With the insistent motion of color, you become silently aware of the deepest self you ever have known yourself to be. Will and mind fly "from things becoming to the thing become," to a world where the temporal has vanished and every facet of change, decay, and beginning is absorbed in the unwinking splendors of eternity. Then the scintillating presences hovering above come crowding upon your head from all sides, filling the air as larger, more human than your neighbors of everyday life. The walls around you seethe in color. Pillars, melting in movement, have no more substance than flames. If you stretch out, you will touch no solid resistance but caress the infinite. If you raise your head too high, you will be assumed into an unknown meadow of God's peace. Of course, architecture, engineering, chemistry, mathematics will tell you a precise story. Many stories. In that sum, you know: the dome of Agia Sophia, all 107 feet of its enclosure, is huge, is predecessor and exemplar for St. Mark's of Venice, St. Peter's in Rome, St. Paul's of London, of Capitol Hill in Washington, D.C. Above and around you there is a clever disposition of shaped stone, colored glass, cunning paint, gold leaf, light, and shadow. Fix a strong, neutral light—an electric arc lamp—on any corner and space of it. Despite all color and shaping: the sight is of dead surfaces, gray curves, nude angles, staring holes. But thus you are going at things backwards. With abstractions as your guide post. And you have blackened your eyes against all seeing. As if those who built it all first assembled the bits and pieces and then perceived the vision. As it happened, they sought in stone and glass and paint merely apt instruments for expressing a prior vision. It is still accessible to you—but not by any abstraction.

If it is daytime, turn out any electric lamp. Let only the light of the sun, however much or however dim, illuminate for you. If it is evening or night, assemble some banks of tall candles, and let their jumping pulsations of light leap for your eyes; or the colored flickering of oil lamps. You will then understand the significance of the old folktale about Kira and see sometimes the streams of light issuing from the city buildings and joining the brilliance from the skies above Istanbul. For even in its latter-day garb as a Turkish city, Istanbul remains the location of the Constantinople vision.

Today it is a humped, hooded, grimy-faced block of human habitations out of which sprout Turkish minarets and buildings like cloaks shrouding the ancient things on the seven hills: the Seraglio Palace, Nuruosmaniye Mosque, Suleiman's Mosque, Mahmud II Fatih Mosque, Selim's Mosque, Mihrimah Mosque, Alti Mirmer, all waiting silently to be transfused with a light that does not come. North, on the Golden Horn in the Fanar district, Greek Patriarch Demetrios looks out with old eyes in a still young face from a shabby little house in a vegetable garden, musing how long more—five? seven? ten? fifteen years?—before the Turks have their way and he, the last symbol of the ancient vision at Constantinople, is expelled. In mainland Greece, Americanization and modernization are taking over changing basic life styles. Throughout the Soviet Union and its Eastern European satellites, the ancient vision is covered in the long night of a totalitarian system which is forcing the bearers of the vision out from the historical crevasse into which their forebears crawled in desperation before the storm. In Western Europe and the Americas, over four million descendants are trying to discover the difference between nationalism and faith. It is still the long winter for the Constantinople vision. A quiet winter of waiting, one feels, for some vivifying touch—the passing by of the Pantokrator, so that the hem of his robe stop the bleeding and mend some inner fracture of soul.

Meanwhile, throughout Thrace and Macedonia and

the Peloponnesos and down among the scattered islands of the Aegean, the ikons of the vision hang in little white-washed chapels. In each one it was, is, and shall be for all the waiting time as at Daphni monastery chapel six miles west of Athens. You approach it today through fields of poppies and tall grass. Built in the fifth century. Seized by French barons in the thirteenth century. Captured by the Florentines in the fourteenth century. Captured by the Turks in the fifteenth century. It became successively a mosque, a powder magazine, a police station, a lunatic asylum, and a sheep pen. Two Frankish sling bolts were embedded in the Pantokrator on the Dome. The last Florentine duke, Franco Acciajuoli, was garroted in the sanctuary by the Turkish Pasha of Thessaly. But throughout all this there remained and still today looks down at you the mosaic of God the Father, calm and serene in utter power, gazing down untroubled by the murder and the violence and the forgetfulness of men, in the repose of stark, plain omnipotence, as though all the centuries and as though every veil hiding the divine from the human were as flimsy as the cobwebs spun by the morning spiders across the lane, mere gossamer that shields the light which once filled men's eyes here.

Outside the stream murmurs between the fields. The crickets are in chorus down beneath the pine trees. Trucks roar on the nearby highway. An Olympic Airways 707 echoes distantly in the sky above. A sports convertible stops at the monastery gate. "It's a beauty. It must be ancient." A woman's voice. "And we almost passed it by," he answers, removing his sunglasses, "let's take a few shots."

5

ROME
Guarantee of Person

Like an ancient vine, the Eternal City grows around an undulating S-hook of the Tiber, as it flows through the Campagna plain from north to south. Clinging to the left bank are seven aging clusters—really seven hills clothed in layers of buildings. On the right bank: two clusters—the Vatican and the Janiculum hills; then westward, suburbs and highways sprawling out over fifteen miles of land which slopes gently down to the Tyrrhenian Sea and the Mediterranean. North, southeast, and east, the city is surrounded by hills. Only to the west is it open.

You will find all kinds of differences between Rome and other great cities. Rome, for instance, alone has a unique predominance of certain earth colors—brown, yellow, slate gray, plum, ocher red, orange scarlet, and that luminous white peculiar to the clouds in these skies of Latio. When the sun shines, it is a city sprinkled with old gold dust. When the sky is overcast, the city seems carved out of unshifting sand dunes. But, over and above all physical characteristics, Rome has one other difference.

Although full of monuments, tombs, and the works and traces of dead men, although lapped in festal mists of memory, Rome alone gives none of the taste of death which lingers elsewhere as a constant accompaniment to all the great monuments of men. If places, like people, convey a connotation of their inner meaning and their value, this is Rome's: eternity; perpetuity in eternal calm; permanence in some elusive power that waxes and wanes, recedes and advances, is there but cannot be seen, is felt but cannot be measured, is trusted, less or more or not at all, but persists always. Those who merely visit there enter unknowingly but willingly into the hush of Rome's eternity as into a choir in suspense. Many depart after a sojourn of some time only to leave behind an indefinable part of themselves preserved in the amber of some golden experience which enriches them for having had it and bereaves them for its ceasing.

Some who go there decide to stay forever. The hush of Rome's permanence takes them over completely. At first, they ascribe this to a sort of reverse immortality. They become enthusiasts for ancient Rome now become sacred to them in its age-old vigil. All Rome's trees and monuments and buildings appear to lie sunk in centuries of ecstasy. An old calm forms itself into the lips of echo for them, stirring from formerly beloved places and things. Even the vagaries of Roman weather do not reach them: the calm of ancient things deadens the wayward whine of the *temporale* winds, silences even the purr of the fetid noonday heat. But their look is backwards: "To live here is to be in conformity with literally thousands of years of history, with the men and women who made that history," wrote Macaulay.

Insensibly, importantly, at some indeterminate point, this feeling ceases to be backward looking. One day it changes, flows into that other dimension of silent permanence that the city diffuses as its very aura. The quest for—perhaps, even the sense of—immortality which encompasses Rome's past becomes forward looking. There is reflected then a new wholeness as in a mirror of eternity. Death, if it intervenes around them, seems, nevertheless, to have nothing to do, properly speaking, with Rome or Romans or with the wholeness of the vision. Over and above the clangor and bedlam of modern Roman streets, incongruously enough, there comes a sense of perpetual calm: the very air seems rapt and waiting breathlessly for a whisper withheld; there is the comfort of a deep silence in which all the brawling of city life is hushed; and through it there drifts the gentle hint of a strange, everlasting secret, announcing all the elements vital for a human being's happiness. Promise for one thing; personal, made by one person to another person. Then love: superb and gratuitous and warm—as all love should be. A guarantee finally: solid and irresistible, that neither promise nor love would suffer defeat or eclipse.

And so has begun the participation of millions, one by one, man by man, woman by woman, in the Roman vision. Without perhaps realizing it. Without any formal religious attachment. Without being history hounds, culture vultures, or archeology buffs. Without breathing a prayer to any gods ever. Without doing obeisance to a pope or confessing to a priest. Without either bowing to doctrine or breach of doctrine, as they kneel in spirit to the nearness of the Ultimate. The strange life in belonging to something which states: "I am. Forever. Stay with me." The freedom enjoyed in something that says with authoritative power: "Do as I say. Believe as I teach. You shall live forever." Their spontaneous acceptance of being loved: "You were made, not for hatred, but to be loved eternally." The Roman vision has thus become theirs— even if only for a while and according to their capacity. At times, they sense puzzling but not necessarily dismaying contrasts. At noon they glimpse the white-robed figure of the pope at the window of his fourth-floor apartments, emerging momentarily as if from some great and wordless calm. At midnight of the same day they can stroll on garish Via Veneto with the weaving crowd of tourists, pimps, transvestites, pickpockets, teenage prostitutes in hotpants, and mincing male homosexuals in skintight silk pants; breathing the warm gasoline-laden air; listening to the roar of honking horns, unmuffled motorcycles, and the cries of nightclub barkers. And they wonder: what is there in common between that white-robed pope as the symbol of a very ancient lineage and the almost orgasmic character of this midnight pressure cooker? Or has all mutuality between them long gone? What, for that matter, is there in common between this official bearer of the Roman vision and that vast pressure cooker of human beings out across continents and oceans? Once the Roman vision was paramount in many places where, today, there is only ferment, febrile changefulness, rebellion, defection, and what appears to be wholesale dechristianization of public and private life.

We first hear of the vision in Rome between 55 and 85 A.D. The men who came with it were, with few exceptions, Jews from Palestine who had known Jesus of Nazareth. They were unique in their time: they changed history. Still for their Roman contemporaries they were much the same as Asians in modern Uganda, Muslims in Hindu India, or Ibos in Nigeria: pariahs, outcasts, the dirt of the streets. What distinguished them—Peter, Mark, and a few score others—was not a hieratic or hierarchic structure or a power structure in any accepted sense, but solely their claim to have the authority of moral power and to rely only on what they called spirit. They put themselves forward as the bearers of a new vision of the human Castle based on their trust in the love and the spirit of Jesus, as they phrased it.

The moderns have an almost insuperable difficulty here. Our minds are cluttered with all the mythic distortions, ecclesiastical touches, and sociopolitical colorations given the figure of Jesus by generations of Christians and their enemies. For us, moral authority spells coercion of free men; and power in the spirit is redolent of multiple, sometimes hateful tyrants of the spirit. We find it difficult, then, to glimpse Jesus as the centerpiece of that vision of Peter, Paul, John, and the others. In their writings and their life styles, we find a portrait of Jesus which followed no previous or subsequent model to be found in the political histories of men, or in their varied mythologies. It is a portrait of one who, though completely innocent, was—by his own decision—punished with extreme suffering and a felon's death; and who having died was—by his own power—gloriously alive and well permanently again within three days after his burial. The first men to speak of the vision spoke of three traits of Jesus: his person, his sacrifice, and what that sacrifice had achieved for each man and woman before and after it took place.

They were insistently personal in Jesus' regard. Before his death—or so they swore—they had, each one of them, lived, worked, eaten, and traveled with him. They knew the color of his eyes, the timbre of his voice, the touch of his hand, the meaning of his glance, his stride, his mannerisms, his eating habits, the keywords of his thought, the sound of his step, and the varying moods of his personality from morning till night. They knew his conversation, his gleaming speech of simple things known wisely, his easy speech of deep things told luminously. They had *known* him. "Whom we have heard, whom we have seen with our own eyes, whom we have watched, and touched with our hands: about him we are speaking," was how one of them put it, over sixty years later. So dear was he to them, apparently, that their days and nights were bright with him and spring filled the three years they spent with him.

After his return—resurrection, they called it—from death, they again saw his eyes and face, ate with him, touched the wounds he had received, heard the same timbre of voice, recognized the same meaning glance in his eyes—not a mere wraith of the delightful years they had spent with him, but his full-bodied living glance, and all the psychophysical traits they had known in him before he died. They swore to all this. Most of them died violently—by beheading, crucifixion, drowning, stoning, hanging—for so swearing about Jesus. Because they were Jews, they called Jesus by Jewish titles: Messiah, Christ, Anointed, He Who Was To Come.

When they spoke of Jesus making a sacrifice, what they stressed in his extreme suffering and painful death was, curiously for our minds, not the suffering or the extremeness of the penalty he paid. And this, not because they were a less sensitive, more brutal generation than we moderns are—never, perhaps, was there a generation so insensitive to others' suffering, so brutalized in their human sympathies, so unconcerned about the yearly violent death of millions, as our own. Besides, for us today the idea of bodily sacrifice—a man or woman put to death by others—holds little significance beyond physical facts: the suddenly rigid and warping figure in the electric chair; the jerking and slumping of a firing squad's target; the quick swish and silent, swinging deadweight of the hanged; the mangled silence of the mugged, the napalmed, the bayoneted. Ours is, in one sense, the age of victims in meaningless sacrifice.

According to those vision bearers, the real sacrifice made by Jesus was inside him, within his mind and will. They described it in a drama of opposites within Jesus.

On the one hand, the serene being and beauty of the divine in Jesus. An everlasting realm, beginningless and endless, knowing neither the visitations of a rising and setting sun nor the variations of seasons, youth and old age, nor of centuries. Incorruptible by pain and tiring and wasting and death. Abode of spirit ever wakeful in the exceeding measure of its own light, ever reposed in the deathless possession of fullness in being, of completion in truth. On the other hand, the vagaries of being human: birth from a woman, growth, striving, paining, tiring, hoping, wasting, and dying. As God, the vision tellers said, Jesus enjoyed the fullness of the divine. As man, Jesus submitted to the human bondage while remaining divine. Thus, eternity and transitoriness. Immortality and corruptibility. Being and becoming. This was one set of opposites; the basis of Jesus' sacrifice. All the others sprang from it.

The next set of opposites, they explained, affected the free choice of Jesus to die or not to die by violent hands. On the one hand: the natural and overriding urge of any human being to resist and refuse the agony and mortal wrench of death as the ultimate evil to be avoided at all costs. On the other hand: his voluntary acceptance and adamantine determination to suffer a painful death. On the one hand: conscious innocence of any legal crime; a totally sinless life; the innocence of holiness itself, of immaculate perfection, of flawless being. On the other hand: death as a public felon and—in divine eyes—death as surrogate act of penance for all felonies, all crimes, all sins; the bearing of that universe of human malevolence as an ugly agglomerate that clung to all the avenues of his senses and thought, clogging all evidence of human good.

Finally, there was for their minds the impenetrable depth of the anguish of Jesus. For them his woe was of one who knew God without need of any inference from intellect and its created shadows of divinity and without any need of evidence even from the richest of things seen, heard, touched, tasted. Yet his pain was more grisly for its mystery than for the blood from his own arteries which stained his skin with the ugly patchwork of a bled body. They ascribed to him the supreme will to gaze forever on the face of God and to view God's inmost being, bathing thus on the acme of bliss.

They told of this woe and anguish in the pithy short-hand of men aghast at the force of will by which Jesus, as lord of his own soul, could retain the sight of his own divine being and yet forbear to take his joy in it. They were obviously humbled by the love which could erect a wall between itself and felicity, could implore mercy from its own fidelity and repeal from its own decision but rein itself from claiming either. Only so would that suffering be greatest because loneliest, they said, and only so would his will be in perfect poverty of joy in heaven and earth and throughout all the range of beauty. For this, they maintained, had been the essence of his pain: all memory of such to be thrust clear of his mind; earth and heaven to lock iron floors around him; so that he grope alone in gloom beneath all zones of joyous being and be lost in wastes of desolation no man willingly visits, and no man leaves once he has ended there.

One part of the story of Jesus in the Roman vision is as unbelievable for us moderns as it was for the Roman con-temporaries of Peter and Paul. It was not the sacrifice it-self; for the ancients—unlike us—were used to the last sweaty, bloody moments of struggling heifers, bellowing bulls, bleating sheep, lambs, and goats, screaming pigs, and wildly fluttering pigeons and doves as the knives, axes, and cords of sacrifice drew life's blood in rituals whose effect was regarded as only momentary. And the ancients, like us, had their "higher" moments of perception when they could appreciate a dying hero, as many of us do today: a brave spirit unappalled by the closing light of his day: his physical being shrouded by the skirts of doom which he faces bravely; powerless then to do anything more than to go and lie forever with others on beds of perpetual darkness in unknowing peace. But, it seems, for the first bearers of the Roman vision, Jesus was not primarily a nobly dying hero, a wonder worker, an inspiring leader, a model for human conduct, an intelligent founder of an efficient organization, nor a preacher of fundamental truths. They presented him solely as the accomplisher of a new status for every human being.

This new status they described as the condition of any human being in the fresh human Castle made possible by Jesus. It was the ability of men or women to transcend the limits of their intelligence and will and senses and bodily strength, making the invisible spirit the source of intellect, its reason and its logic making moral commitment the operative basis for physical strength and all sensory deployment. Only a guarantee of eternity and immortality could attract men to transcend themselves, said the visionaries. That guarantee, in their eyes, was a living Jesus: "You need have no fear of losing yourself. A man, who was divine, died, lived again, and will live forever. He promises you the same eternal destiny as himself." It was this living warranty of immortality that they announced as the kernel of their vision. "Unless Jesus rose again from death," wrote Paul, "what we are saying is sheer rubbish." And it was this which remained ingrained in their memories: the unshaken will of Jesus to abdicate his joy; to bear the trophies of his physical punishment imperially; to be puddled in his own blood, but—before a hand was laid on

him—to be self-doomed and self-sacrificed; and to do so as
the permissive master of his own fate.

It is no wonder then that their extant descriptions are
full of echoed memories of how Jesus had shown himself as
the natural king through all his weeds of loneliness, lacking all acrimony. They tell in simple terms how his manhood was mangled for man's infidelity, his flesh and skin
and hair and limbs were torn and stained with blood.
Now, they said, it would flow as soul's baptism through
the wide world. And even those who never shared their
beliefs were and are taken by the pathos and beauty of the
image they presented. They told of Jesus' sacrifice as one
that could not be earned by humans—only accepted or
rejected. They said: it was offered by gratuitous love
which gives seed to all love, generates all compassion, is
the substantial home of all reason, the chamber where all
light echoes. They told of the deep change effected by
Jesus in all human beings. According to them, the change
made all of them human, even as it guaranteed that they
always had been so, and that they could not be less or
even fathom what to be less might mean. And because of
this death of Jesus which they saw pinioned forever between his life and his living again, the human bondage was
broken; immortality transformed and transfused mortal
beings; salvation was a fact of life; the human Castle was
here.

That those far-off men believed in what they announced is borne out by their lives. What is not easy to
explain by arguments drawn from sociology, politics, culture, psychology, or human power centers is the success
of their Castle vision. When Pe⁻ r and his companions
(some as prisoners) came to Rome, there was no human
hope at all. They had nothing: neither armies, money,
support from a military power, social manifesto, theory of
government, sympathetic lobbies, culture, nor friends in

high places in Rome or abroad. They even had no desire
to fight or labor for any of these things. They never had
an armed revolt, never sought financial or economic hand-
grips, never achieved powerful lobby support with the
centers of government. They were not interested. They
had only that vision. And when their successors did succeed two hundred and fifty years later, it was not because
they had acquired all or any of those things in the meantime. They had not. Peter, himself, bluff, Judaic, of
strong temper and a still more powerful love, died crucified head down. He was nobody for the wide world of his
day. He, his contemporaries, and his immediate successors relied only on the force of their commitment to spiritual power and moral force—alien terms of action for our
day, although many today mouth such terms.

Neither in early Christian writings between 50 and 350
A.D. nor in contemporary records is there any facile and
obvious explanation to account, on a scientific basis, for
the emergence of a victorious and dynamic community of
men and women whom both Jews and Romans tried to
suppress, the Greeks laughed at, and Constantine had to
acknowledge. And, at moments when we relax our ever-
present fears of being duped by myth or fooled by
superstition, we do feel the most obvious explanation is
possibly, even probably, the true one: those men had a
genuine power of spirit and exercised a moral authority
with the consent of free men in their day. In 100 A.D.,
Christians numbered not more than 5000 to 8000 centered
in various cities of the Near East and Greece and around
Rome and Marseilles. By the time Christians came to the
fore in the sophisticated Roman world of 400 A.D., they
were everywhere: in all of Turkey, Greece, Bulgaria, Rumania, Yugoslavia, Albania, Palestine; they comprised
three-quarters of Italy and Spain, one-half of France, some
parts of Belgium and Germany, about one-fifth of Britain;

they had permeated large coastal stretches of Africa. They numbered millions in the fading Roman Empire.

In our diverse and variegated modern world of burgeoning nationalisms, developed localisms, and instant knowledge of the human tapestry, it is difficult to realize what a homogeneous world the Roman world was. For centuries, Rome had been the center of it all: and Romanitas the norm of humanness: finance, law, culture, literature, politics, social and family life, religion, class structure, folkways and mores; all methods of civic administration—public works, intercity transport, security, taxation, property ownership, military defense and offense; education, learning, cosmetics, clothes, domestic cooking utensils and farm implements, buildings, mosaics, music, painting, hair styles, accents, plumbing, hygiene, graceful living. All was homogenized, blueprinted, mass-produced, identical, according to the models adopted in Rome. Romanitas was the polyvalent and universal standard. We have no word for it. Into the intricate arteries of this entity, the message of the Roman vision—its faith and its commitment to spirit and moral authority—poured without haste, taking centuries in fact, and without violence.

But it took hold of men amid a growing desolation of human power in might and glory, flourishing at a time when the city of Rome, from 350 A.D. onward, entered a long thousand-year decline. Fire, earthquakes, disease, invasion, neglect, poverty, civil wars ravaged its ancient magnificence. The population diminished to a median of 30,000 to 50,000 and was concentrated on the Campus Martius (near the Vatican Hill) and in what is called today the Trastevere district. The ancient buildings were plundered for materials: marble, mosaics, granite, columns, lead, bricks, blocks, and plinths were filched. Grass grew in the streets. Pavements buckled. Some of the sewers ceased to function. The aqueducts fell into disrepair. The metropolis became a ghost town as debris, dirt, dogs, dung, desolation, and dinginess clung to the ruins and skeletons of imperial Rome's priceless architecture where now thieves and muggers abounded and a miserable population scurried and scavenged. Only grim reminders subsisted of the former temples, market places, courts, altars, triumphal arches, shopping arcades, artisan centers, military barracks, theaters, colonnades, public baths, senate house, palaces, villas, gardens, fountains. And at the city's edge, on all sides, there ran miles and miles and miles of cemeteries: funerary monuments, statues, mausoleums, vaults, tombs, and common graves. Not until Pope Sixtus V (1585 to 1590) would the resuscitation and beautification of Rome be genuinely undertaken.

In the middle of this growing desolation, we find the successive bishops of Rome standing as the representatives of Jesus and as guardians of the vision. The bulk of evidence we have concerning the first ninety successors (up to the middle of the eighth century) confirms the judgment that their primary concern was to exercise a spiritual and moral authority and to spread the knowledge of the Roman vision. The highlight of such an exercise is provided by Pope Leo I (440 to 462) who saved the city from Attila the Hun. Attila was poised (452) to attack and destroy Rome. There was no army in all of Italy to save the city militarily. Leo rode out alone on a mule. Talked with Attila. Attila withdrew. This is so mysterious for us today that we seek all sorts of scientific, rational, psychological, even medical explanations. None accounts for the reality: the force of moral power in the spirit. Attila and his troops were in that state ascribed by one historian to the Russian divisions on the eve of their final assault of Berlin in 1945: "A ferment of hundreds of thousands of men, hardened by months of killing, burning, looting, raping; brutalized by blood and explosion and death, reduced to almost animal conditions of dirt, hardship, daily danger, and ferocious hatred of man, woman, child, animal, and even of living trees, and led by commanders who, with their men, thirsted just to be let loose on the heart of their enemy." Anyone who has been among an army on the eve of an assault can understand such a ferment. Today, a rough equivalent of Leo's achievement would have been afforded if the Bishop of Berlin walked through Unten Der Linden and turned back the Russian armies and their commanders. So difficult would it be for us to understand such an action that, if it did succeed, we would find many explanations other than the moral force and authority of the spirit.

Because of the same gap in understanding, the centuries between 450 and 1000 have been called the Dark Ages—both by theologians basking in the metallic glow of medieval reasoning and by historians writing and commenting from the pseudo-brilliance of the Century of Lights. For to a man of the 1700s with new physical discoveries breaking around his eyes every decade, the quietude and calm tenor of that earlier period appeared to be backward and unenlightened. Of course, science had virtually stopped. Humanistic literature had long declined. The arts did not flourish. As values, these had long ago lost any power to rescue man from his human bondage. In the circumstances, they had to decline. Under the tutelage of the Roman vision, the men and women of Europe were engaged in a far more serious business: defining the confines and the value of their humanness within a fresh paradigm supplied by the Jesus of the Roman vision.

The vision provided a fresh and encouraging persuasion about man in his universe. The ancient world had been haunted by only one surety: that man is, or can be, noble, but perishes forever into nothingness. This was the sum of all that men had been taught by Greek philosopher and poet, by Roman sage and Jewish prophet, by Gallic legend and Iberian sage. It had been a world governed by what Gibbon called the "terrible twins": strength and weakness. Strong wills and weak wills. Enlightened intellects and dull intellects. Beautiful bodies and ugly bodies. Delighted senses and blunted senses. The elite and the masses. Free men and women and slave men and women. And at the end, the dust of corruption and the common oblivion of the grave. Human living was a closed arena with one common exit. The ancients did not attain our degree of factual knowledge; but they outshone us in reason; and they taught us logic. Yet all this brilliance gave them none but these alternatives.

The message of the Roman vision opened something new, and was quite clear. A crucified god became the centerpiece of the European world, assuring all men and women that they would live forever, that they were loved beyond the grave. Belief in this took effect on what lay deepest in the human heart. All human life was made to link up with that belief. From symbol to symbol. From imaged action to imaged action. From analogy to analogy. Until the arms of the Crucified embraced the whole world and the whole of any individual man or woman. Everything human was evaluated in its light.

A human being was great not because he overcame nature or because he discarded it, but because his human nature had been sublimated. A human being knew his humanness not because he could be great or do great things with it, but because he could be greater than it, could transcend it. He acquired a speaking glance for his fellow man and a meaning look for life. Human destiny ceased to appear as misfortune or death. The world ceased to be a chaos of "terrible twins" as the men and women of that age discovered their inner order and its reflection outside them. The drift of the stars became a meaningful pattern. The earth became a shadow play of men traveling, not a void but an ordered path.

Within the quietude of those centuries were laid the foundations of medieval philosophy and modern science. Even with the slashing attacks of Vikings and Norsemen, the wars of barbarian remnants, the Muslim onslaughts of the 700s, an inner peace and stability of spirit established and maintained itself, creating a race of men and women inwardly assured, outwardly in harmony. At this distance, even in their prosaic and simplistic manners they appear to us as "bound for somewhere," a race to whom the map of life was clear.

By 1100, the promise of the Roman vision had seemingly reached so far into the marrow of that people, and the confidence in immortality gained through Jesus was so much a fact of life that the vision began to take on visible form silhouetted against the human landscape of Western Europe. The Gothic building has been described as the plastic expression of that Castle vision: Salisbury Cathedral—Blake's "Heaven's arrow on the plain"; the Duomo of Milan (Matthew Arnold described it as "the iced cake of Gothic"); or the trispired cathedral in Cologne, pithily called "a human promise" by Goethe. The Gothic church was designed to house the mystery of human immortality: the sacrament of Jesus, centerpoint of any such building, was for those people, his presence among men immortalizing their mortality, sweeping their spirits forever to the infinity of life promised. The Gothic style appeared two hundred years before men were versed in the subtleties of reason and logic, five hundred years before Federigo Montefeltro announced the Renaissance saying, *"Vogliamo essere humano"* (we wish to be human). It required few of the secrets uncovered by the physical sciences seven hundred years later. But Gothic would have been impossible without much harmony-full love of a savior and trusting hope in a promise that in order to be human, a human being had to have a greater than human destiny.

Even for us—exact-minded and minutiae-filled earthlings that we are—when we walk in these places today and look around us reflectively, a bell still rings in some immemorial niche of our memories. Some magic casements open on to seas of feeling we first fear because they are unwonted. We walk between walls that bear no weight but rise up and dissolve vertically, cooperating with each other upward in solid thrusts of hue and stained glass and subtle carving. We have to resist positively or be taken captive by vertical radiations in arch and line that begin above us emanating from the air, by facades that become transparencies of colored sunlight, portals that lead inward below successive ribs of molded mastery, leading us inward ever farther to the sanctuary and the altar while growing freely upward through an increasing multiplicity of views and a recession of dovetailing vistas on to ever-beyond rims of sight and to depths beyond those rims. For here is substance in flying structures: each part of this whole is not separate and lost. It is united and permanent and found and identified by the grace of a greater union impossible to each single piece. No matter how you try to remain earthbound, the building will carry you upward by a simple stratagem: like you, it is part of solid ground, the good earth, but rising—and you with it—to meet a lofty goal. It is your aspiration, you aspiring, in stone. Your desiring self, not measured against an overbearing skyscraper height or a mothering mountain breast, but borne aloft. Your gravity made celestial. And you cannot really resist, because it is all done at your human rate of speed: starting slowly with the gravamen of prostrate pavements and feet-deep granite walls and deep thrusting foundations in dark crypts; then, unnoticedly, picking

up speed with quickening inner details, even as
the mechanism within yourself, of all that makes
you human, starts to convolute; and finally all of
the structure—and all inside you, desire, awe, expectation, instinct, curiosity, fear—are gathered up weightlessly, spiraling heavenward soundlessly in a final breakneck never-turning-back bid at the skies above our world.

This calculated weight in tons of stone, brick, cement,
wood, plaster, marble, lead, iron, and glass is not sitting
four-square solid *down* on the ground. All as one, one as
all, each part because of all the others, all are pushing
upwards, rising as one toward the sky, all made volatile
and aery, pouring the invisible essence of their skyward
thrust in silent strength through the interlocking arteries
of ribbed vaults, climbing arches, flying buttresses, lacing
cornices, beveled eaves, up and up and up into the fluted
spires and fragile turrets, slim-pointed, delicately balanced, aimed like space rockets of a more esthetically
minded race of astronauts, lovingly chiseled skyships
always about to race for a wanted zenith, for some silent
height of human yearning to be of this earth and to live
here with the immortality man always dreamed existed
beyond his mortal span.

Its builders and worshipers were more specific in
their desire: to house the sacrament of Jesus' presence,
mirroring the immortal permanence they expected from
his love.

It all mirrored the ideal of the human person which
was formed then: one who could believe reassuringly; one
who could feel hopeful; one who could look down at his
own clay because God had come of clay and still aspire au-
thentically to outlive that clay's mortality because his savior was divine; who was morally responsible to Jesus for
his actions and religiously responsible to Jesus for the
well-being of his own self. The Christian person was

thought to have a wisdom, a mystic gnosis, which gave all: ennoblement, happiness, surety, strength, beauty, access to eternity, and, above all, power in spirit and by spirit to develop all his human traits. It was the type of human being celebrated by Dante at the close of the medieval period: one held in a vision of eternal beauty and harmony. It presumed the constant existence of eternal pain and irredeemable ugliness and the eternal order of being which ranged everything from lifeless stones and invisible atoms up to the highest order of archangels, within the sanctifying gaze of a loving god become man for love of all men and women. It was a poet's vindication of what the third-century Christian writer, Tertullian, had written about the effect of Christianity in himself: "Having a divine savior, I am human. Nothing human, I reckon, is alien to me." This was the inherent promise of the vision: all things human would be sanctified in its eternity.

Already by the eighth century, Christianity had formed the seeds of a great culture, a new epoch of civilization. Inevitably that time of tutelage drew to an end. In the 1100s, we find Europeans budging from their historical grooves: land and sea explorations; the start of scientific experimentation at Oxford, Cambridge, and Paris; the arts beginning to flourish; new and developing lines of intellect and reason. All perfectly natural. All supremely human. The Europeans were awakening once more, once more on the move outward, ever outward, intellectually, geographically, artistically, poetically, industrially, demographically.

Ideally speaking, the official bearers of the Roman vision should have relied uniquely on Jesus as the supreme model of humanness. They should have adapted to the new circumstances of a vastly changing world by means of the complete flexibility of Jesus transcending time, space, and all human changes. For they had been told, they said, that in his name all things human could be sanctified. And so they had been assuring men and women for centuries. But, ironically in human terms, by the time the first rib was thrown across the vault of the first Gothic arch in 1093, a compromise had been made with the Roman vision. Genuine flexibility was foresworn. The consequences of the compromise were not felt then, as the momentum of the vision carried forward. Effected around 800 A.D., the compromise would take over one thousand years to play out its implications. But in it the human Castle of the Roman vision was thrown awry.

It started with Leo III, Bishop of Rome in the eighth century. He felt threatened. Islam, within a space of one hundred years, had swept over once Christian lands—Syria, Lebanon, Palestine, Egypt, Iraq, and all of North Africa. By 750, Muslims owned all of Spain, had penetrated into France, occupied Sicily, and eyed mainland Italy. Leo also saw a threat in Constantinople, the most magnificent city and imperial center men could imagine or had ever heard of. Its Eastern Orthodox Church and its Patriarch possessed the most glorious and highly developed part of Christianity. Learning, culture, art, music, graceful living, prosperity—only in Constantinople were these to be found in such proportions. The Patriarch and the Orthodox church claimed to be next to the Bishop of Rome and his Latin church; to be, in fact, of equal status with Rome. Very few men in the West knew Constantinople well or understood intimately the beauty of its vision. Lastly, in Rome itself, Leo was in trouble. And here he was indeed threatened. For some time, the Bishop of Rome had become the sole civil power levying taxes, punishing offenders, taking sides inevitably in civil and political issues, both in Rome and in recently established papal states of Corsica, Venetia, Istria, and elsewhere. Leo became so hated that his life was in danger. In

799, he fled to Paderborn and took refuge with a new northern power: Karl the Frank or, as he is usually called, Charlemagne.

Charlemagne now became the chief transforming factor of the Roman vision. Charlemagne, with his six-foot four-inch frame, his blue eyes, his walrus mustache, his squeaky voice, his unwashed hose and perpetually worn shirt, his total inability to write even his name, his prowess in battle, and his dream of being the new priest-king of God's kingdom in line with David and Solomon (Charlemagne saw them as Christians before Christ), Charlemagne was the ready answer to Leo's prayer.

The contrast is stark between Leo I in the fifth century riding out on a mule to stop Attila the Hun and his army, and Leo III in the eighth century running off to Paderborn to secure Charlemagne's knights and lances.

Charlemagne's plans were grandiose. They sprang both from ignorance and ambition, as well as from his religious beliefs. In his eyes, the Roman vision with its promise concerned exclusively the only church he knew, the Latin church, with its Roman center. In his eyes, *Romanitas* and *Christianitas* were identical. He knew no better. Aix, modern Aachen, his capital, was to be a second Rome: his imperial chapel was octagonal after the model of the Holy Sepulcher in Jerusalem; there was a building there called the Lateran—to parallel the Lateran palace of the pope in Rome. His throne was modeled on Solomon's (Charlemagne planned to be the successor to Melchizedek and Justinian). His court was called *sacer* (sacred).

Leo, completely steeped in power play, had equally grandiose plans. Here was the perfect foil for Constantinople's ambitions, Leo concluded; and with his Franks, his Lombards, his Anglo-Saxons, and his Celtic mercenaries, a bulwark against the Muslim menace. Leo crowned Charlemagne emperor of the West on Christmas

Day 800 A.D., throwing himself at Charlemagne's feet in reverence and respect. Leo had now not merely committed both his office as Peter's successor and guardian of the ancient vision to a Western power, he had alienated one-half, the more ancient half, of Christianity—in the name of military, political, and economic advantage—and he had made Christianity a Western thing. The results were incalculable.

Leo's move made Christianity an exclusively Latin affair and a Western phenomenon. Constantinople broke away from Rome, refusing to be Latinized. Christianity's fortunes were tied to the Western mentality such as we have known it up to our own day. All the military and sociopolitical prejudices of the Carolingians were taken over and made marks of Western Christianity. There appeared for the first time an officially pursued doctrine of the Roman popes according to which the safety and propagation of the Roman vision depended on the secular government in any country being organized according to the political instructions of churchmen: the "confessional" state. As an inevitable corollary: the force of the vision's moral commitment and teaching was placed in civil laws. To say the least, there was no longer reliance uniquely on the power of the spirit.

In that era, also, hatred of the Jew, of the Muslim, indeed of any non-Christian—and that meant for the Carolingian mentality any non-Western European—became standard, approved, even holy. We are still living on Carolingian ideals in education, in logic, in city living, in law. Even the Carolingian idea of woman is ours. We still nourish the Carolingian contempt for easterners and southerners. We still regard the Mediterraneans and the Greeks as somehow or other unreliable. Our world is still ruled by the Carolingian division of Europe into the cultured West and the uncultured East, the logical and clear minded versus the Byzantine and the obscure (sometimes, more complimentary, we speak of the mystical). It is a division which took on new life with the Cold War of 1945 to 1970.

Leo's decision locked all activity of the official vision bearers into a power stance. The figure of the sacrificed and resurrected Savior, centerpiece of the vision, became an imperial and authoritarian overlord intent on political domination. Henceforward, all that Rome did, preached, founded, supported, opposed was dictated principally by the desire for power—political, economic, and cultural. The strength of the spirit was interpreted as temporal influence. The church became a politicking church with autocratic demands and conditions. The essence of spirit became synonymous with domination of political life. Church leaders sought on all sides every possible means of fostering such power. And there started the papacy's erratic gamble for political stature in this world, which went on unremittingly for over one thousand years, until 1870 when the pope was stripped outright of all power. Even in 1929, when all hope of former influence was gone, the papacy still demanded the trappings and status of a tiny state.

Serious as all this was, it was but a reflection of the deepest damage done. That was to the flexibility of the original vision. Briefly, the Roman spirit stopped in its tracks about the year 800, ceasing to draw on its vision for renewal, for furtherance, for enlightenment, for enlargement. The new attitude absorbed all energies. The original "gnosis," the spirit knowledge supposedly won by Jesus, was no longer developed. Merely contained, rendered static, tied to the formulations, opinions, ideas, theories, and the mentality of pre–eighth-century European man about the vision. In fact, those ideas and formulations were no longer seen as attempts by minds of that time to express the vision and its spirit, its gnosis. On the contrary, "spirit" and "gnosis" were statically identified with those ideas and formulations. Social slavery, serfdom, the unjust division of rich and poor, the status of women, married love, these and other basic human questions were never asked. For all the power and panoply that were attached to the papacy in ensuing centuries, the long-range results were disastrous. The church taught men to reason through its philosophy schools and introduced them to the physical sciences. But it was all meretricious. In the static view of the Roman mind, it was held that all reason and research should merely bolster its traditional standpoints on all and every thing. All social, humanistic, political, and scientific progress was tied to the imprimatur of a cleric who claimed power over all.

It was a sham. And the sham wore thin. By the late sixteenth and early seventeenth centuries, men turned their developed critical faculties on the church and to the material universe of man. Of course, they found much to critique and an ocean of misinformation, prejudice, superstition, and error in the traditional viewpoints of churchmen. But the Roman church authorities could not listen. They had shed their own belief in moral authority for its own sake and deriving from Jesus, together with the original flexibility. Their poor replacement, their autocracy, was at stake—in science, in philosophy, in morals, and in politics. It was too late for change after eight hundred years of staticism and protectionism. The Protestant revolt was inevitable and logical. The break with scientists was due. Once you link spiritual power with temporal, both the spiritual and the temporal are up for auction in the mart of power politics and economics, surpassing in degree if not in kind any corrupt money changers on the steps of an ancient synagogue. So deeply ingrained had the power stance in the Roman church become that its leaders went into a state of siege which lasted all the way from the sixteenth to the late twentieth century.

Today, almost 1200 years after that first definitive compromise, the present claimant representative of Jesus and guardian of the Roman vision, Pope Paul VI, ten years in office, now 77 years old, wrapped about with his isolated dignity and responsibility for the vision as with watchful presences, this man surveys Rome, Europe, and the world from high above St. Peter's Square. How judge him, the guardian? And how assess the vision?

One thing is clear and certain: Paul is presiding over an inner decadence of the political Church structure started in the eighth century. An inner decadence and, barring miracles, an unavoidable decadence. Inner: because the very innards of that structure have melted; gone is the obedience of people to priest, of priest to bishop, of bishop to cardinal, of cardinal to pope, that cohesion built on absolutely accepted dogma and affecting the daily life, personal decisions, and intimate thoughts of millions. Unavoidable: because as a sociopolitical structure it no longer appeals; it is out of kilter with the fashion of mind, the bent of will, and the social development rife among the nations who once fitted snugly into the one-thousand-year-old solidity of the ecclesiastical church. That was a juridical church, a pyramid of power: its high centerpoint, the papacy, was the center of gravity, creating all stability, distributing the weight of authority down its sides to the broad base. All efforts, its external policy as well as its internal discipline, were invented precisely to foment a juridical structure. But it was a contradiction. Today, power no longer flows down from the apex. The broad base of the pyramid is dissipating itself, crumbling, spreading out over the vast plain of human affairs. And there is no recall of the ancient juridical solidity. Foreseeably, a day is coming when there will no longer be a sociopolitical structure such as the Roman Catholic church has been up to now.

As for Paul, no world figure is more besieged than he, no world leader more troubled by those he leads, no pope more unpoped than he. Outwardly, the titular head of this tiny Vatican fiefdom; outwardly, too, the chief administrator of a church which is officially numbered in the six hundred millions; his is an elfin voice overheard at times only like wind wailing at dusk in a lonely valley. Bearer of Peter's vision and Leo's mistakes, responsible in his own mind for that vision to the Jesus of the vision, gripped by leukemia which is slowly eating his life away with the leisure of the sure and slow old man's killer, Paul's mind is gray with problems he will never live to see solved, and his days are occupied with managing an organization where the spirit no longer dwells. The organization provided the vision only with a bureaucratic labyrinth to live in and a juridical bed to lie on. Daily Paul bites into the same crust: his secretaries come with their lists and decisions and then go; Cardinal Villot, his Secretary of State, conducts the policy discussions; Monsignor Benelli, his other familiars, bishops from every diocese of the world, Vatican officials, privileged visitors all troop in with obeisance, recount their problems, solicit day-to-day solutions. The reports pile up: already, the damage to the structure is irreparably far gone. There is no escape for Paul from the iron thrust of crisis: not a screaming storm, and not a wildcat fire; only the irreversible advance of affairs—beyond his control—to a brink over which he cannot peer.

With one of the best-organized and most plentifully supplied sources of constantly refurbished information at his disposal, Paul knows that he exercises only a diminishing moral authority and power in the spirit. He is beset by the grave and unreturning issues of the last negotiable moments in the life of the ancient Roman structure, that structure within which the vision was lethally coffined. He is helpless as the Roman vision begins to incarnate itself in a totally different form before the rest of the world.

Ten years before Paul became pope, the Roman vision had already begun to seek other channels. There had been for over twenty years, and increasingly in the last ten years, a new development in the Roman Catholic Church. It is as yet only scatter shot in character, traceable only in isolated happenings and unexpected manifestations: tentative efforts, sometimes wild experimentations with almost totally negative results; new, highly vocal groupings of hitherto submissive and silent parts of the church; attempts at new formulations and methods of worship; free-wheeling independence from clerical control and ecclesiastical supervision; a constantly more plaintive, but strong, protest that it is spirit which matters. Throughout it all, with all its variety and sometime insanities, there runs a common theme: the search to find a suitable mode of expression for the invisible and intangible but nonetheless real commonality in spirit and moral practice which, they believe, Jesus accomplished as the patrimony of all men.

There is here a dovetailing of the Roman Castle's development with the radically changing human environment of today. For, in the Roman vision, the power of moral authority and of the spirit derives from Jesus and not from political structures; and it requires another human environment, of which only the merest beginnings are to be found today in the fragmenting reality of human beings—mechanized, routinized, tormented, rebellious, searching, as they are, but wonderfully charged with excitement. Never before, as far as one can judge from known history, has there been such a leavening of all mankind, a melting of all man-made barriers, so that the divine can manifest itself and the Castle vision become a shared thing among all men and women and children. Foreseeably, throughout their planet and in each locality, they will be utterly indistinguishable one from the other and no longer specified by the particularisms and prejudices that have hitherto divided them. For such an environment, it was proclaimed at the beginning, the Jesus of the Roman vision came. And this is the only human situation which promises further life for that vision of the human Castle: humans pulsating in all directions with heightening awareness of the spirit as distinct from the body; wearying instinctually of all psychological substitutes for inner morality; impatient with dead heroes, transitory wonder-workers, indeed, with any leader who is merely clay as they themselves are; and insistent—sometimes frighteningly so—that their humanness be guaranteed by some force and power which does not share the mortality and the weakness of all things human and which will guarantee the human person as inviolate.

6

PEKIN
Everyman an Ex-Palace

The Pekin vision of the human Castle, the newest of all such visions, flashed out before the eyes of the wide world in 1966. The day was August 18. The place was the one-hundred-acre *T'ien-An Men* (Gate of Heavenly Peace) Plaza in Pekin. At the Hour of the Tiger, well before sunrise, the plaza started to fill up with one million young Red Guards, brought in from all over China. As they assembled, up from their shuffling, restless, ever-spreading numbers there arose what was at first merely an eerie murmur. It grew in naked volume as the masses swelled, until the voices of hundreds of thousands welled up as flames mounting to meld with the heat of the sun as it peered over the eastern horizon.

Precisely at that moment, Mao Tse-tung, his arm supported by a nurse, emerged on the upper gallery of *T'ien-An Men* Gate. And, suddenly, the seemingly impossible: no sound. Just for a fraction of a second. Then, a roar of thunder lashed out deafeningly, a bullwhip of adoration and fury. So the Cultural Revolution (or, literally, a "full-scale revolution to establish a working class culture") was born within all men's hearing.

Curiously enough, Mao's physical appearance is no more impressive than his name (literally: Hair-Swamp-East) as he shuffles around in his soldier's olive green uniform. He is slightly above five feet in height, hump-shouldered, stooped in stance, running to flesh around the middle. Nor does the face beneath the muffin-shaped military cap ("potato faced" is one observer's epithet) have one impressive feature or configure an impressive power. But this is the most powerful man on the face of the earth today. He has decided the interim fate of over eight hundred million Chinese. He may also be the man with the greatest say about what sort of world all men and women are facing.

But at the age of 72 on this August day, Mao is above all else a desperate man. We in the West may be the last to understand Mao Tse-tung's goal. We have great difficulty in distinguishing between the physicality of any given human situation and the untouchable vitality of the human spirit. We can no longer understand the fanatic or the zealot; nor do we give them any genuine credence. Not only us, many of Mao's own entourage have been, and many still are, repeatedly mystified by his "ventures": his Hundred Flowers Campaign and his Great Leap Forward (both in 1957) and his Socialist Education Campaign of 1962. His objective, he said, was "to educate the new man and to reorganize our revolutionary ranks." But the net result of these seems to have been a weakening of the Chinese Communist Party (CCP) and disruption of China's economic and social life. Why the destruction? Why shatter the solidity of the sacrosanct CCP, remove its leadership, and send pangs of turmoil through China's millions?

On the speaker's stand, Lin Piao is stumbling nervously through his words: "Chairman Mao is the most outstanding leader in the present era. . . . Mao Tsetung's thought is Marxism-Leninism for remolding the souls of the people. . . ." The crowds of youngsters are in a delirium at these words. Mao goes down among them. A girl student from Tsinghua University drapes a brassard around his arm. It reads: "Red Guard!" The rhythmic chant goes up: "Mao Chuhsi wansui! . . . Chairman Mao ten thousand times! . . ." Another speaker repeats a phrase used ten days previously by the Central Committee of the CCP: "The Great Revolution now unfolding is a great revolution that touches people to their souls." Is this "touching people to their souls" merely a phrase? Or has it some more-than-symbolic meaning? Marxism with its dialectical materialism denies any soul to a human being. Until now, any revolution fomented by the disciples of Marx and Lenin had as its aim to undermine the capitalist system throughout the world. But to "touch the souls" of the Chinese people?

In the afternoon, Mao descends again to chat with the Red Guards. They tell him their problems: "We are not allowed to have our souls to give," is one complaint. He tells them: "We must declare war on the old world." And subsequent events will show that this "old world" is not capitalism or the capitalistic West, but something in China itself.

Throughout that long day, Mao did not make one speech. He moved around slowly, listened intently to the various speakers, waved to the cheers, smoked incessantly. Only after the last firecrackers had exploded did he step into his limousine and leave the plaza, pursued by the rhythmic chants: "Mao Chuhsi wansui! . . . Chairman Mao ten thousand times! . . . Mao Chuhsi wansui wansui! . . . Chairman Mao ten thousand times ten thousand times! . . ."

And in the next 24 months, these cheering Red Guards will turn China into a great spastic body racked by civil disorders, destruction, killing, public outrages, vandalism, hunger, cruelty. The CCP will be a shambles. Eventually order will be restored. But in 1973, the new Party Constitution will endorse Mao's principal doctrine of "continuous revolution in the Chinese people." "For a long time to come," Chou En-lai will state in 1973, as an explanation of Mao's vision, "there will be two-line struggles . . . 10, 20, 30 times." This policy of Mao, this Marxism, is unrecognizable as classical Marxism-Leninism. In that theory, certainly, the Party will finally disappear—but only after it has installed the Paradise of the Workers. But it is unthinkable to destroy the Party's strength before its work is done. Yet this is what Mao has done. And what he proposes to do continually. What sort of vision, then, has this man?

The Pekin vision is the soul child of Mao himself. He spent fifty years pursuing the classical Marxist-Leninist ideal. Only at 63 did he clearly see his vision of the Castle. Only then did he come to know of the slavery which has held the "souls" of the Chinese people locked into a two-level world almost since the time that David slew Goliath with a slingstone.

The Chinese Empire was put together by Chen, ruler of Ch'in (hence the name China), a northwest state, between 229 and 221 B.C. In its heyday, the Empire's achievements in culture were impressive. But for the individual person, the story was much less glorious. Symptomatically, China produced only moralizing teachers as practical guides for the spirit of its people. Confucius (551 to 478 B.C.) taught the all importance of *Li:* what should be done in order to fulfill one's personal, social, and political obligations. These were determined by one's place in a classified—almost ciphered—society. Mencius (372 to 289

B.C.) taught the "Mandate of Heaven": the ruler had a license from Heaven to rule—as long as he succeeded. If he failed, the Mandate was withdrawn. By contrast, Hzün Tzu (330 to 235 B.C.) held that "all men are bad," adding that "they all need guidance in order to observe *Li*." A pattern now emerges: moral education is the key to moral integrity. Moral authority was authority imposed from an outside source—the ruler.

China was leavened by Taoism, a way of looking at the universe and of understanding how it worked. All was fluid, unceasingly changing, composed of *Yang* (the positive) and *Yin* (the negative). The individual is passive, is acted upon. At about the same time, Buddhism arrived from India. It inculcated the need to forsake all individual desires and to seek a condition in which the individual is swallowed up in a transcendent wholeness.

From the fusion of Taoism and Buddhism into Confucianism, there arose an all-pervasive philosophy of life. The cosmos was held together by an unchangeable law of flux: the supreme *Li*. All had to conform to it. China and its emperor were the center of the universe. All were held in a totally impersonal system of hierarchical elements running from the utterly negative all the way up to the utterly positive. It was a simple system of endless being.

The only meaning for the individual came from the "wholes": family, village, community, county, state, province, kingdom, the Empire, China, the universe. "Man," said one early Confucian, "is like lice in the fold of a robe. Heaven no more listens to him than he himself would listen to an enquiring flea."

All humanness and all individual identity consisted of conformity to *Li*. Humanness had no dimension of innerliness. The individuality of each person was not something inviolate and personal to him or her. "Sin" was an offense against good behavior exteriorly, but it had no inner correlate within the individual. "Spirit" was roughly equivalent to our "consciousness." "Heaven" was a portmanteau term for the way human life worked out.

Within this system for thousands of years there developed China's world. In political and social terms, it was essentially a serfdom of millions ruled by the few. For those few claimed to have a special privilege: to be immune from the nonhuman meaninglessness of the masses. It was, thus, a two-tiered world. On one level, the laborious mass of mere things: people, animals, plants, inanimate matter, all that simply is. None of it really human. On another level, the privileged few who constantly became more easeful, grace filled. This was what it meant to be truly human. The ideal was to belong to that special group who could avoid labor, the sweat of the many: the Sons of Heaven. The system was reproduced physically, in almost its exact image, in the Forbidden City of Pekin, that far-off residence separated from the dreary fate of all other mortals.

For about fifty years of his life, Mao's ideal had been to take that Forbidden City—and all it stood for. And he had been schooled in the rigid materialism of Marxism-Leninism as developed in Soviet Russia: merely to transfer power from former masters (the Kuomintang) to new ones (the CCP) would do the trick. He had been indoctrinated in the Soviet Marxist frame of history: just let the Party rule; the Paradise of Workers will ensue. Fired by these principles, he had lunged out of his northern mountain fastnesses in 1946, overrun mainland China, and triumphantly entered Pekin in 1949. All power and wealth had indeed been seized. Nothing escaped the CCP's control. Approximately thirty-three million Chinese had been liquidated; and, six years afterward, over eighteen million Chinese were sweating in labor camps. The Forbidden City became the Ko Kung, the Ex-Palace. Now its visible possessors were the Party and the People. And was not that the goal of the Revolution?

But Mao changed; his vision of the Castle became complete. It was the sheer physicality of his own regime which opened his eyes. From 1949 onward, the CCP and the People's Army (PA) had been in complete control. Throughout China Mao saw the emergence of an elitist corps, military and civilian: the *apparatchiki*. Arrogant. Power-laden. Authoritarian. Holding the population down by absolute control of all means of life. Something deeper than his understanding told Mao that his regime, as it was developing, was bound to reinstate and congeal the twofold slavery of Chinese souls in an unholy pyramid of power. And over westward, he had the prime example to reinforce his intuition: the U.S.S.R.

The physicality of it all struck fear into him. After a mere six years of supreme authority, the CCP was degenerating into a bureaucracy and a power clique as rigid, ritualistic, ineffectual, and totalitarian as the old imperial Mandarinate. But he had not merely fear. He also had an intuition of something infinitely precious—the human person—which in all Chinese history was never honored and never had a voice.

Mao has never claimed a revelation from a "beyond"; and he has never indulged in philosophizing. Rather, he claims to be the voice and the mirror of the masses: "Direct your eyes downward. Do not hold your head high and gaze at the sky. Unless a person is interested in turning his eyes downward, he will never in his whole life understand the things in China." His vision seems to have arisen from a feeling for China seen in a perspective which transcends both time and space.

It is as though he had etched upon his mind the screens of K'ang-hsi or one of the panoramic landscapes painted by a master of the T'ang or Sung dynasties when they celebrated some renowned beauty spot, though Mao transposes the details in terms of our Third World: an ever-growing majority of nonwhite people; a vast majority of men, women, and children who go to bed hungry each night and rise each morning in prefabricated despair; a vast majority of mankind living in conditions like those that obtained in England and Europe somewhere around the end of the fourteenth century.

An artist of such old panoramic landscapes is at once poet and painter. The very movements of his drawn shapes emit color. For days you follow him across fields, through valleys and villages and caverns, over mountains, along roads, and by river banks. All appears flowingly uniform. And yet all quivers quietly.

You begin to perceive the infinite two-level scene: a fragile fabric of finesse draped ever so lightly over a fluid mass of semihuman reality which forever thrusts upward. Its desire is to be free, to be fully human, fully itself. But it never closes the ineffable gap that separates it from the "upper" level. It is fated to stay covert. And this is what China embodied for the Chinese eye and mind during its multimillenniar course: a city of beauty and privilege held by invisible powers over a primal precreation lump of non-selves, nonpersons riven with striving, locked in defeat.

You perceive all this in stages. First, here and there, little half-finished cameos leap out playfully at you: the zigzag branch of an apple tree, for example, looks like a petaled finger stiffened at the end of a sentence you never hear. Little by little, as you stand back and take in the scene, you discern on one level, the painted silk is convoluting into wisping mementos of protean being forever forbidden to be integral: unlikely mouths without a chin line; azoic lozenge eyes above no nose; streaking eyebrows on a shaven forehead which unaccountably recedes into the blank surface of inarticulate matter; half-faces that started to smile before you looked, but never finish the smile as you glance; willow patterns of arms and legs, fingers and toes, all writhing and thrashing silently on unseen torsos; breasts, buttocks, navels, and ears sprouting from the friable soil.

The whole scene is given as an unsuspected and tongueless world of rustling life aching to signal its existence, but so ashamed of being what it is and so impotent to assert itself in any human fullness that it forever scampers for concealment from your search. In Chinese culture, this was the fate of the masses: always to be without the dignity of an independent self.

Over all this is laid that other world of privileged humans, and we can see it as Mao's thought imaged for us on a lacquered screen—an artist's concept of the Few anywhere: the CCP in China, the Soviet leaders, the minorities who decide the fate of the masses in India, Africa, South America. The artist depicts them as brilliantly dressed, fitted with limbs of near translucence, gravity free in their movements, and outlined in an elongated grace that recalls Blake's etchings and El Greco's saints: but without the unearthliness of the one or the disortion of the other. Their world is imaged as the finest of gossamer silk, lying airly over that "lower" level of other than genuinely human beings. Always, those privileged ones move above it all on their own plane, as if they share a huge cosmic joke: that ordinary life is an illusion because the delicacy of distinction is forbidden forever to the mass of the people. They, the privileged ones, were quite free from the restless serfdom, the anonymity of things cemented into the ageless Wall of Being.

When you "revisit" such a scene and see it with the eyes of Mao Tse-tung, a strange realization dawns on you: Mao's vision is about the human person, the individual self, today about to be liberated, so that each can be his own self. It is about the masses as the very source of new inspiration which will show men how to effect that liberation. He utterly trusts in a new historical happening, the Revolution, a sustained process with a dual movement, what Chou En-lai calls a two-line struggle. One line: the continued efforts of the organizing few. The other: the continual eruption of the organized masses. With each eruption, the rigid position of those few privileged ones is frittered and shaken. The whole process of ongoing eruptions is a slow but inevitable change in roles.

In these terms, Mao's vision of the human Castle is complete. It is not merely that the Forbidden City becomes the Ko Kung, the Ex-Palace. It is that each individual ceases to be forbidden to be a human self; that he be allowed his innerliness. But, according to Mao, there is a power in the masses which, in world history, has never yet been released. When the time comes that it has been— through a series of spasmodic eruptions—the individual will be fulfilled, and his fulfillment will be the fulfillment of society. Mao has made his Chinese comrades pay a terrible price in the valuable coinage of their humanness—the very thing he envisions as their noblest possession: he has put the beast of Marxism-Leninism in such a privileged position that there may be no dislodging it.

Nevertheless, this is the terminal point of his vision: the new man. "Criticize and reform your selves," he has instructed them all. "Sit down and mobilize your souls." Mao uses "soul" when speaking of culture. But this is not the *psyche* of Aristotle nor the *anima* of the Latins. And today, in Mao's China, you will meet young men and women telling you, with unfeigned enthusiasm, that they now have a soul or a new soul; that they are now really Chinese persons; that they have something inside to live for and some personal light for their minds. Mao Tse-tung, for all his cruelty, has given them their inner selves. For the first time, the Chinese have been told that each one has an inner self which he must cultivate and identify. It is a big first in the long history of China. Mao is a K beyond Kafka's wildest imaginings: he has assailed an ancient palace, not to live there, but to dismantle it stone by stone and to build instead a Castle not even he can see in detail.

Whether we like it or not, Mao has etched mankind's problem in frightening colors: how can a human being be an individual with his own soul and not fall into the egotism of greed and the solipsism of pride? How can he love himself—and others? On the other hand: how can a human being be organized with others and not become, thereby, a cipher, an ant among many other ants, and thus lose his soul, his individual identity? How can he love others—and himself?

The awesome aspect of Maoism is not merely that it has underscored this central problem in the abstract. Mao has provided one answer—right or wrong—for the majority of men and women today.

And so, having momentarily shed on the world of his time the questioning intuition gnawing at him, having provided the Third World with one solution for its pain and want, and having spilled much blood of his own fellow men, Mao—no different from any other man—is about to depart into the long unending night of death, the last of the great individual leaders in this age of confused little men. The whole world of mankind, which must go on for an unforeseeable cycle of unknown tomorrows, will not easily lose sight of his words: "I am alone with the masses." These, as the purest grains of his egotism, now cling around his old man's shoulders as he slips away. Behind him, he leaves a trail of dark questions beginning with this: What will mold and safeguard a man's innerliness?

Evidently, neither nationalism nor social ideals nor a political cell nor the Communist Party—according to Mao. But something coming from the soul of man and from the souls of the masses. This, in Western terms, can only be divine. And hence the ultimate puzzle of Mao's vision. For he has repeatedly referred to his own death as "going to God." But what real communist ever believed in a god or a hereafter? After Mao is buried, it is the masses, always alive when the Great Ones of history die, who will still be here, alone and still awaiting the Castle of their hopes.

7

ANGKOR WAT
Smile of the Self

In the Tower Chapel of Angkor Wat Temple, two
hundred ten feet above the courtyard, King Jayavarman
VII of Cambodia stands surrounded by his officials. All
about him is a galleried complex of corridors and terraces,
each terrace rising above another to the uppermost court
where five towers reach for the sky. It is within the chapel
of the highest of these towers that the King stands. Over
to the northwest and connected to Angkor Wat (Ang-
kor=great; Wat=temple) by highway and causeway shim-
mers his capital. Unique in all Asia, Angkor Thom
(Thom=capital) is surrounded by a moat ten miles long
and one hundred yards wide, with four central gates, and
a fifth—the Victory Gate—in the east wall. The balus-
trades of the bridges are lined with six-foot sandstone
giants carrying the bodies of Naga serpents.

   Outside its walls and moats, there gleam artificial lakes
and reservoirs connected by canals lying between towers,
all mirroring balconies, roofs, carvings of temple facades.
Myriad temples: the Baksei Cham Krong tower dedicated

to Shiva; the three-towered Phnom Krom; the Buddhist Prah Khan temple with its 20,000 images of gold, silver, wood, and stone; the Bahaka Horse in the middle of Neak Pean Lake; and more, always more—Prah Neak Pean, Ta Nei, Banteang Samre, Lolei, the pink sandstone Banteay Srei (The Portal of Women).

Within the walls of Angkor Thom, clusters of buildings rise. They rival the splendor of the Roman Forum and the Athens of Demosthenes: the Phimeanakas Temple, the Prah Palilay Towers, the twelve-towered Prasat Suor Prat (The Towers of the Tightrope Walkers), the Tep Pranam Buddhist Monastery, the Royal Palace roofed with painted tiles of lead and clay, the Terrace of the Elephants, the Terrace of the Leper King.

On this day, a continuous river of people stretches from the Royal Palace in Angkor Thom all the way over to the main courtyard of Angkor Wat Temple. All are still, gongs and cymbals held silently in their hands, faces turned to the Temple, waiting. They had come in sunrise procession—Jayavarman and his officials in the lead setting out from the Royal Palace, a mass of men and women and children in gaily colored clothing passing in the lightening shadows of palaces, halls, statues, monuments, bridge towers, shrines.

The royal procession—soldiers, nobles, elephants, courtiers, people, and their King—reached the West Tower Gate of Angkor at a slow pace. Within, king and courtiers passed over a ten-yard-wide road of flat paving stones, the Causeway, laid out in a perfectly straight line, five hundred twenty yards long. At the end, the sun, which had just risen behind the temple, had become a stream of red and gold glory pouring over the five towers of Angkor Wat, splashing into the persevering traces of night darkness. From the Gulf of Siam a freshening wind blew landward.

For those instants of processional walk over the last five hundred twenty yards, the Temple as it appeared to the eyes of the approaching worshipers was the five-peaked Mount Meru, the golden mountain where dwelt the Divine, the Absolute, Brama. All, in fact, Temple, terraces, towers, lakes, capital, moat, all this is for them a visible microcosm of the invisible macrocosm: the Divine dwelt there on a quincunx plain; around the peaks revolved two suns, two moons, two sets of constellations. All was enclosed by the vast Ocean of the Milk of Immortality. Beneath lay the world of serpents, of devils, of evil spirits. "My walls pierce the sky with their pinnacle," is Jayavarman's comment in the inscription which has come down to us; "my moat reaches down to the unplumbed depths of the world of serpents."

Here we find a quality unique among all Asian lands: there is no fear, not even reverential fear. On this spring morning, in this greening land beneath a blue-streaked sky, the smiling gaiety of the crowd and the grace of the buildings they built seem to be mirrors of a wonderful smile. These are the Khmers, and it is the year 1198 A.D. They are not about some animal worship or engaged in sacrificing to magnificent idols. It is the Day of the Smile and the Spring Feast of the Enlightenment of Lord Buddha.

High in the Tower Chapel, the King sets a watcher to look out from the window to the northeast in the direction of the Neak Pean Lake where the statue of the Sacred Horse, Bahaka stands. Bahaka, in Khmer belief, carried the souls of the divinized mortals across the Ocean and over the Rainbow Bridge of Indra, to Heaven on Mount Meru. Before dawn, a ceremony—an enactment of this Bahaka liturgy—was begun. Once done, a signal was relayed to the Tower Chapel.

That signal come, the King and all around him turn

toward a statue: the Lord Buddha with the face of Jayavarman but with a dim and incomplete smile. The eyes of
Buddha are blank; the smile itself has no meaning glance;
there is no self to be seen in that blankness; and no human
smile is appropriate in response. All is potential, hiding,
waiting to be evoked. An official hands the king two
golden pins now. Quickly and deftly, he drills holes in
those blank eyes of the statue. An artist steps forward.
With swift strokes he dabs in the irises and the eye lines.
The effect is instantaneous and almost magical: the smile
on the lips is woven into the newly open-eyed glance and
envelops the whole face. It is now truly smiling, almost
laughing. It is as if the smile of Buddha-Jayavarman leaps
from its face to the King; as though the human reflects the
smile of the divine, and the divine shares the animation of
the human.

The smile of the statue leaps to the King, to his officials, to all. The Chapel gong breaks the silence; and the
sound as the echo of the smile booms musically across the
countryside sparks replicas of sound along the river of
gongs and cymbals come to sudden joyous life in the
hands of the crowds. Faces turn and voices are raised, to
laugh and sing back at the Smiling Buddha, the symbol of
their identity and their joy in living.

The Smile of Angkor Wat.

That smile and the vision of the human Castle that
evoked it shone only in this one corner of the vast Garden
of Buddha. The smile was symbol and substance for the
vision which had a triumph greater than any other vision
known to us. For in that Garden, where to be human was
to be doomed, this sudden smile was an undoubting and
joyous assertion of the individual, a celebration of the
worth of self and a vision of that self living forever. Only
here in Cambodia and among the Khmers and only for
some hundreds of years did wildly exultant tunes of gypsy

music waft the message: "So good to be alive!" The smile conveyed: "Even better to be human!" The art by which they expressed their beliefs and faith proclaimed: "Best of all to have the Lord Buddha's Enlightenment enriching our living, filling our humanness."

By way of contrast and to heighten the achievement of the Khmers, we should remember another and a totally different ceremony that took place on the same day. In Buddhist monasteries all over the rest of Asia monks sat within their walls in seclusion. From the broad band of Asiatic Russia, down through Mongolia and Tibet, China, India, Burma, and Southeast Asia, all are as those in, say, Ajanta. Here in the assembly hall of the monastery buried sixty-four feet in the bedrock of the valley wall, some two hundred miles northeast of Bombay, each monk sits cross-legged. Saffron candles burn quietly, almost unwaveringly in the unbroken silence, their incense pervading the air. It is just another day in the life of those in solemn and rigorous quest for the Enlightenment of Buddha.

In the immobile face of each monk, each pair of eyes is closed; each mouth is slightly open, pursed, and drawn; one could not quite call the expression a smile, rather a faint trace of lines appearing at the corners of each mouth. Every head, unseeing, is lifted in the direction of a colossal statue of Buddha cross-legged and shadowed in velvet tranquillity. Its eyes too are closed. Its mouth is as the mouth of each monk. The abbot barely breaks the silence to instruct a novice in prayer: "Through vipasana you become liberated from all that is human. The self will wither in you. You will break the cycle of rebirth, and reach Nirvana. Renounce. Renounce. Life is a prison. . . ." The smile on the face of this Buddha statue is meant to capture emptiness. Not as a goal or bridge. Merely as emptiness. It is, paradoxically, a vivid portrayal of nothing. The smile, expressionless in its fixity, remains a narrow, curved space between two lips through which all, to the last inconsequential, undesirable atom, has been breathed out slowly into a beyond of unmentionable silence.

It would be a pity if in our knowledge of history and the story of mankind's visioning we failed to take notice of so great a difference. On the one hand, the transient glory that inspired the Khmers of Cambodia to reflect in their carving and their building and in social works as much hope as is expressed in any medieval angel, as great an ideal for the human person as celebrated by any Renaissance humanist. On the other hand, an expression of hope disenfranchised in the human heart and a will only to evacuate rather than to celebrate the self. It would be a chance at human understanding missed if we did not ask what can account for the transformation of Khmer civilization and the daily life of the Khmers into such vivid colors that for one brief moment in 6000 years of Asian history it stood out in such arresting contrast to all the ways of life in all the lands around it. What made Buddha smile at Angkor Wat?

Behind the smile of Angkor and the not-quite smile of Ajanta lies the same key: a mysterious and, at this distance, an almost unknowable character. He was born Siddhartha around 563 B.C. How and why he came to be called Buddha, or the Enlightened One, and before his death (487 B.C.) to be the founder of a great world religion is the great mystery of his life. But two elements seem to sift clear of the legend, myth, fancy, and theosophy woven around his name: his revolutionary character and stance; and his supreme personal experience so powerful and profound that it changed him and thereby changed the lives of some few billions of men and women.

Siddhartha's world was Brahmanic, and it was Hindu. Brahmanism, the oldest religion in India, was already in his time encased within idolatry and laced around with legends of fear and danger and servility. Hinduism was a religion of excessive cruelty, worldly ambitions, and a numbing asceticism. Siddhartha rejected both as blind alleys that did not lead to the divine. One is inclined to speculate that in another day young man Siddhartha might have stolen a headline or two from young man Luther. But such would not have been his intent; for it can only have been the personal experience he underwent that was the wellspring of all his greatness. Sometime before he was 30 years old (at age 29, if we are to believe the accuracy of the *Mahaparinibhana Suttanta*), Siddhartha underwent the experience that transformed him and which, some fifteen hundred years later, would transform an entire people, the Khmers. They would cut through the dry methods and systems of mere rigor and in a flash of intuition capture the meaning of that experience of Siddhartha's.

But we can speak of that event only in images. Every star of the spirit eludes our direct gaze. But through lowered eyelids we can glimpse its glory as it passes by; we can just catch its shimmering as its reflection sparkles silently over the pavement at our feet for moments of such delicious brightness that we can only nod dumbly in response. "Yes" may be our fullest response to the infinite compassion of such a moment of perception. But if we veritably live that moment, our "yes" will not be verbal or even mental. We will *be* the "yes" to a kiss blown to us through the opaqueness of the flesh and the matter of our universe. But always we will experience spirit indirectly.

Siddhartha himself experienced spirit, not by indirection, but confluence: his spirit flowed into and was melded with the spirit. It is a generally agreed upon opinion among writers and students that the confluence was between two: on the one hand, the substance of Siddhartha, the substantive self he was—thinking with his mind, desiring with his will, imagining with his fantasy, feeling with his senses; and, on the other hand, the spirit, the divine—not a remote and condescending and visiting deity, but a plenum of conscious being swaddling and thereby sustaining in its immaterial ether all particular beings—in this case, Siddhartha.

This supreme moment was preceded by an onerous striving on his part. We know that he labored to eliminate from his mind and memory all the fanciful myth making of Brahmanism. This effort must have left him in a state of looking and waiting; of straining to empty his mind so as to put something there. In such a state of mindlessness he found a fresh illusion. Looking at the darkness he was inducing into his own consciousness and trying to discern the dawning of light, splitting his consciousness into thoughts and thoughtlessness, then breaking himself once again on the thoughtlessness and splitting this latter into a new illusion, immersed more fully than ever in the puzzle (a puzzle that has very modern echoes) of how to know without mythic knowledge, and subtly reasoning how without logic he could arrive at a conclusion. We also know that he worked at eliminating all the psychic convolutions, all the acrobatics, of Hindu mental asceticism.

But at some moment he stopped all the subtle gyrating within him, all the tiring quest not to be tired, all the endless trailing efforts to get rid of himself. The clash of psychic gears ceased. He was no longer the febrile initiator. Another, the Other and the Greatest, had come, was present, fulfilling everything; and everything had been and still was emptiness. His own self still was, and was still emptiness. The darkness did not cease to be darkness: it was now seen only as the light reflected in what had had no light. It was clear because what mattered was clear. Everything else was in emptiness. And all was compassion.

The moment lasted no time; because if it had perdured, within it he would have passed away. And it lasted longer than time; because within the paradigm of timelessness (which he had reached) there is no beginning which heralds an ending and no ending to any beginning.

What we glean from the records about this moment pulls us up short. Appreciated in its purity, it can arouse in us an inner pain of nostalgia: we sense our nearness to our true and only human home. That spirit, as it confluenced with Siddhartha's spirit, enveloped him as an infinite condescension, compassionate and loving, absorbing in infinite perception all his capacity to perceive and in its infinite fulfillment all the fullness of desire. At those rare moments in life when time stops and an infinite instant yawns around us, we have remote analogies to Siddhartha's moment. Because in such a state there is no vividness in any one of the senses and no physical movement, we imagine all is asleep and emptied out of activity. And we come to confuse the state in which that spiritual moment occurs with its touch and with its *purpose*. We come, for example, to imagine that the *purpose* of Siddhartha's efforts was nothingness. We ourselves sometimes experience in our consciousness temporary and apparent "sleeps" of mind and will, a vacuity that bores us; but this happens because our sources of knowledge and desire come through our senses, and they sometimes tire of giving.

In the Enlightenment of Siddhartha, there was no such quietus. There was no dormancy of mind or evacuation of will. The mind cannot sleep from perceiving: it *is* perception of what is desired. The will cannot cease desiring: it *is* desire of what is perceived. Rather, for the first time, his spirit was fully active: his mind was totally filled, his will completely satisfied in its desiring, his memory locked in actual possession. For instants or for an instant—probably the latter—the divine touched him directly, embracing him, filling him, satiating his spirit with the ultimate mysteries of being, of love, of truth, of beauty.

It was an instant of love prolonged interminably because there was no way of measuring it. It was ecstasy without a cry of amazement and without a groan of "too much!" There was no final scream of the self preserving the self, and no sigh or moan or resignation to overpowering glory. It was pleasure unsearing, brightness unblinding, warmth unburning. It was peace without sleep and calm without vacuity. It was knowledge without concepts.

There was no more hope, because all that he could hope for was his. Nor was there any faith, because he was possessed by and in possession of all he believed, hoped, loved. All his life he had known himself as an incarnate desire for fullness, for the Paradise of ecstasy. Now, in that Paradise, that self aching with desire ceased to exist. In its place merely the substantial self of Siddhartha in the repose of fullness (as expressed in the records) "without caste, unaffected by smell, without the sense of taste, without feeling, without form, without hunger, without pain, without sorrow, without joy, without birth, without old age, without death, without body, without karma, enjoying an endless and unbroken calm."

Once it was over, for the remainder of his existence its afterglow permanently illumined the features of his conscious mind and active will. The divine compassion with its love and with its light never left him. From beyond the rim of his consciousness, that light of the divine had shone whitening every cliff of his mind in clarity, vesting all the valleys of memory and every field and peak of desire in consummation. Ever after, even when the magic moment of Enlightenment was over, flecks of that luminescence embellished his consciousness like the rays of a sunset that cling to a land long after the sun has disappeared. And the love of infinite compassion warmed his spirit continually.

He could never again be as he had been. He was now Buddha. The Enlightened One. He was already beyond the corruption of living and cured of our principal human failing—self-seeking egotism. This condition which, according to Buddhism, mortals only attain after death in Nirvana, was his while alive. Buddhists have always called it Siddhartha's Parinirvana (pari = equivalent to; Nirvana = emptying out).

Of course, Siddhartha returned to normalcy of sense experience, mental discourse, memory recall, and decision making by his will. But all he could recall with his memory of that experience or at least all he could describe was a great gap, an emptiness within: he had been emptied of fitful desire and all that went with such desires and preferences. And all he could now construct by reasoning was no reasoning; all he could imagine of what had happened was a nonhappening; all he could desire with his will was, ostensibly, no desire, nothingness. For it was under these conditions that the fullness of all being appeared to have flowed into him. His intuition must have been that the conditions themselves had been the result of the spirit's visit. He concentrated on reproducing those conditions in himself and others as mechanically effective means for obtaining enlightenment. Hence the mechanics of Buddhism: the Eightfold Path.

After his death, and on the basis of those mechanics, there were generations of men and women who willingly underwent a deprivation of their humanness which some of the strongest spirits find impossible. As is always the danger, the mechanics, the rules, the means, the formulae, the visible, indeed, the intended means occupied the place of the end they were devised to achieve. Millions of men and women became monks and nuns over the centuries. Thousands of others retired to desolate places, eking out bare existences with beggars' bowls or in lowly jobs, disciplining their minds and bodies, banishing the self, despising the world and life upon it as obstacles to absence of all self, all life. They took refuge in the forest clearings of Ceylon, the silent Himalayas in Bhutan and Nepal, the wind-swept moonscapes of Tibet, the rocks of Japan, the sleepy jungles of Malay and Burma. In modern times, they created little ad hoc solitudes even within New York, San Francisco, London, Buenos Aires, and Montreal.

These were and are the places of their sojourn. They waited and watched and hoped. For long days and endless nights, keeping a faithful vigil for years that consumed their youth and manhood, expectant that Enlightenment would visit them and transfuse their nudity of spirit with a cloak of dissolution, so that they could be one with the All and all in the One. They not only reduced to a stark minimum the exterior circumstances of their lives— clothes, food, dwelling, social life; they also stripped their inner life of all adornment. They subjected their minds to a desolate and bare landscape from which all reasoning and all memories were banished as criminals. They immobilized their wills with the ligaments of prohibitions like heavy irremovable chains. They emaciated their five senses by a starvation diet which excluded any stimulus, any pleasant combination of heat and cold, hard and soft, liquid and dry, loose and tight. For them: only the Path. Right views. Right aspirations. Right speech. Right conduct. Right livelihood. Right effort. Right mindfulness. Right contemplation. The Eightfold Path.

Sometimes, in the darkness of years spent in that rigid training, one of them would be touched transiently by the spirit: the eternal and the infinite bent down compassionately from inaccessible bliss for precious instants to imparadise their loneliness and constancy. In the vast majority of its adherents, the maximum result was a general rectitude of conduct—the Buddhist way of life with its inner establishment of peace and detachment from the world.

The biggest casualty in this development of the mechanics of contemplation was the self. Not merely the inner self each individual claims to be, but the self in its need for social and humanitarian structures. Burned into men's memories of Siddhartha and insistently transmitted to all his followers was the imageless recollection of his experience, when his inmost desiring self was satiated and ceased to yearn and to ache with desire; when, in retrospect, it seemed to them that this very self ceased. This memory seemed to contrast sharply with the desires of normal men and women which led them to strive and suffer throughout their lifetimes. How difficult for them to grasp the image of the cease of yearning, not in nothingness, but in fulfillment beyond all yearning! Instead, it seemed that the desiring self of everyday life was all there was, and that its demise and burial in nothingness was the most desirable aim. That it should be breathed out as a gulp of bad air never to be inhaled again. With it could go the tangle of egotism: frustrations, evil thoughts and evil actions, the kick of sexual desire, the bite of ambition, the misery of ignorance, the cruelty of misunderstanding—all exhaled into nothingness. And this is literally and metaphorically what the word nirvana means.

For most, when the spirit does not come (as surely has been the case on a large scale; there has not been another Buddha), there is only the stillness and rigor induced by the mechanics of inner discipline. The self then is almost certain to be bedded down with disaster. It is pinned aridly in the astringent of nonaction, nonmovement. All is absence. There is peace, the peace of separation, of detachment from all that is humanizing, the arid peace of desolation. And solitude, the solitude of inertia. And certainty, the certainty of mechanically controllable breathing, of concept chains, of memory links, of methods and rules and formulae as substitutes for the touch of love.

It was in this form of inner mechanics and ensuing inner desolation that Buddhism spread over the Asian land mass. Not as a protest against the roughness of human fate. Nor as a proclamation of hopefulness and of man's defiant will to be greater than when he started or secure from what threatened his existence as a human being. But as a refuge from it all, an escape quicker than physical dissolution from the traditional boredom of the ever-grinding Wheel of Existence.

Life, announced the Buddhists, is an endless repetition owing to your passions: the Green Snake of your Desire, the Red Cock of your Anger, and the Snub-snouted Pig of your Ignorance, all three are locked jaw on tail in a sequence that is as ever-returning and boring as breathing the air in and out of your lungs. The Wheel never runs down. You yourself are caught in a merry-go-round corruption. The self you are is a trap. Your only solution is to escape it, to be exhaled as a breath which never returns, and so to achieve nothingness. For then the All will be all there is.

Even when the original form of Buddhism—called Theravada Buddhism or the Lesser Vehicle—was mitigated into Mahayana Buddhism or the Greater Vehicle, the total effect was the same for the self. Actually, today, in round figures, there are only fifty million Theravada Buddhists (in Ceylon, Burma, Cambodia, Malay, mainly); and only seven percent of India's millions are Buddhists in any sense. The majority of Buddhists in the world profess Mahayana which is more "human" than Theravada: there is some mitigation of the mechanics, the loneliness, the hopeless aim of life.

It cannot be surprising that Buddhism on the whole

provided no stimulus for the natural sciences, nor gave birth to any great developments in medicine, dentistry, orthopedics, or mental health. Agriculture, industry, banking, commerce, civic philanthropy, urban engineering, poetry, music, painting, prose, international relations—all these and similar areas whose object is betterment of the worldy and human conditions lay outside the orbit of interest of Buddhism as it spread over the whole of Asia like a benign parasite living off its host. It effected no fundamental change; rather it adapted itself to each area, requiring only tolerance, blending alike with Hinduism in India, with Taoism and Confucianism in China, with Shinto in Japan, and with a multitude of animisms throughout Mongolia, Southeast Asia, and Indonesia.

Buddhism has had no practical effect either on the scented Malay gentlemen sipping their midmorning aperitifs in the sidewalk cafes of Petain Road and Eng Hood Street of Singapore or on the peasants in Thailand, the herdsmen in Mongolia, or the Untouchables at Chouri, India, who still live like serfs and are killed or die like dogs. Those touched and caught by the Eightfold Way—the mechanics—seek to ignore all worldly needs and miseries along with all worldly pleasures. And those who are not so touched and so caught up are left unaided in their agonies, uncompassionated in their aloneness. Katmandu, Nepal, has open sewers in the streets where naked children wander and mothers sit breast feeding their babies night and day, picking the festering scabs of their mosquito bites. There is no one to repair the *stupas* of the Punjab or the 5000 pagodas of Mandalay and Pagan in Ceylon.

For when all the economic and social evaluations and all the five-year and fifty-year plans are done; after all the international aid has come and gone and made no change, the great x of the riddle remains to be faced: what change in life can there be, and what effect can be sought, when the aim of life is to break away from life, all life; never to be born again; then to reach Nirvana.

Nowhere except in Cambodia and in the Empire of the Khmers centered around Angkor has Buddhism so transformed a society, directly enriched it with social and cultural benefits, touched it with a glory, or inspired a desire of transcendence and fulfillment of self. What special vision of the Castle gave these people their impetus and confidence? Who were they? What happened to make their vision unique?

The people involved—the Khmers—lived on the plains surrounding Tonle Sap Lake in Cambodia. They seem to have been indigenous to Cambodia but to have been invigorated by Brahman and Hindu migrations from the West and Northwest, with a strong admixture of Negrito and Malay from the South. Yellow skinned, dark haired, small nosed, mesocephalic, short in stature, narrow waisted and broad shouldered, they spoke a language which (unlike others in Indochina) was polysyllabic; and they used a script derived from India. When they emerged from historical obscurity at about the fifth to sixth centuries A.D., their culture was built around fundamental Brahmanism. This was a religion and life style imported into India about 2000 years previously. It was a remarkable and cohesive viewpoint according to which the universe, the macrocosm, was centered around the five-peaked golden mountain, Mount Meru. Here dwelt the Divine and the Absolute. And here lay the master plan for all the building and all the splendor of Angkor Thom and Angkor Wat.

For the purpose of man on earth was to reproduce a visible microcosm of the heavenly macrocosm, to reproduce it in his buildings, in his images, in his actions. It was precisely this visible reproduction that could serve as a bridge for man to his own self value and to immortality. Everything in this world, men included, had its magic moment—its span of visible existence—and its magic place. The cosmos was controlled by the stars of the Divine and through them were decreed man's allotted place and time. The more macrocosmic—the more conformed to Mount Meru—one became in this life, the greater a chance one had of being divinized after death and of being transferred to the ranks of the blessed who lived with Brahman. Failure to achieve this identity during life meant only that you were reincarnated in some other living form; you were not ready for the heaven of Mount Meru.

Every mortal who could be associated with the divinity had an appointed place among those blessed. Even before he died, he enjoyed invisible privileges. The individual was thus seen as somebody at home in this visible world which, together with the higher world of the divine and the lower world of demons, made up the macrocosm.

This was the fundamental Brahmanism of the Khmers. It had been lightly leavened with stray strands of Buddhism by the sixth century. But the teachings of Buddha never gained any real prominence until the beginning of the twelfth century. The Khmer people were strongly attached to nature cults—animisms and fetishisms; and they peopled their visible world with spirits, gods, goddesses, and invisible forces. Their life style, their art, and their folklore were continually fed from Java where the insignificance of the individual and the fearfulness of the invisible world were dominant traits of religion and politics and personal life. From all we know, Cambodian Brahmanism and its ensuing Buddhism might have developed as elsewhere—but for two men of genius. Both were called Jayavarman.

The first, Jayavarman II (802 to 854) will always be one of the most enigmatic men of history; we will never explain him to our full satisfaction. Of Javanese origin, reared in Brahmanism, a skilled strategist and a thoroughgoing statesman, this distant character seems to have had a power of synthesis worthy of genius. By successful campaigns, he united the two warring parts of the country (the Dangrok mountaineers of the North had always been the enemies of the lowland Southerners). On them all he imposed a political unity. He moved his capital to the North where it was safer and more remote from Javanese influence. Then he set to work on his grand design, initiating the great building tradition of the Khmers and establishing literally a new way of life.

On his invitation, a man called Sivakaivalya, about whom we know little more than that he was a Brahman scholar, came from India as royal chaplain. He was charged by Jayavarman "to establish a new ritual, in order that Cambodia might be no longer dependent on Java"— the words on the Sdok Thom stele which records the life and achievements of Jayavarman II. True to his Brahmanism and faithfully imitated by his successors, Jayavarman set about reproducing Mount Meru visibly in buildings and monuments. At Kulen, his capital and earthly microcosm of Mount Meru, he built a terraced pyramid temple. In it he ensconced a *lingam*, a phallic symbol of Siva. None of this was new.

But his innovation was revolutionary and astounding: it was nothing less than the propagation of a new belief expressed in a special rite. He, Jayavarman, would be identified with Siva. The *lingam* would be called by a double name, a combination of his own name and that of the god. In this way, the divine resident of Mount Meru was now resident in its microcosmic form at Kulen; and he, Jayavarman, was personally identified with that god in the macrocosm just as he was in its microcosmic mirror image. He thus shared in the god's immortality and blessedness.

Thus, Jayavarman's successor, Indravarman, set up his own *lingam* under the name Indresvara (Indra=Indrevarman; isvara=Siva). And his successor too, and on through the years, until the names of the Cambodian kings, each a combination of the human and the divine, ring across the centuries that separate us from them like a polyphony of variations on the same theme: Jayavarman, Bhavavarman, Indravarman, Yasovarman, Rajendravarman, Suryavarman, Vayadityavarman, Harcavarman, Jaranidravarman. Each such image thus set up was called a *dharma*, or sacred monument. Each was the king's personal passport to immortality. "Guard this *dharma*," runs the inscription which Yasovarman (889 to 910) put on the god images of himself and his parents, "which for me is like a bridge to Meru."

Behind Jayavarman's innovation burned an original intuition of the human self. It was new and foreign to the area, unknown in India or China or Japan, even repugnant to certain traditional standpoints. Jayavarman said, in effect: "No one is necessarily condemned either to the endless cycles of reincarnation or to the unloving claws of a cold eternity. On the contrary, you can have worth in this life and perpetuity of life after death—on condition that in this life you identify your self with the Divine and the Absolute." Competent linguists tell us that, although Khmer had no word corresponding to the English "person," Khmer inscriptions use a term drawn from Brahmanic literature which is roughly equivalent to "an inhalation of breath," an in-breathing. It is this in-breathed element—breathed in by the divine, accepted by the worshiper—which Jayavarman declared to be the source of identification with the Divine, the "bridge to Meru," and the fount of immortality.

It is no exaggeration to say that all in Cambodia was once organized around this Meru paradigm of eternity and was concentrated on an all-absorbing building campaign. Through it, they believed, mortal men and women acquired a cosmic dimension: he or she became identified

with the deity and associated with the mythical Mount
Meru. Indeed, Jayavarman changed his own title to "King
of the Mountain."

For almost six centuries, successive kings before and
after Jayavarman II shifted the capital city around (we
know of at least nine sites: Prasat Ak Yom, Kulen, Ro-
luos, Trapeang Phong, Prah Ko, Bakong, Lolei, Siem
Reap, Koh Ker). But from the tenth to fourteenth centuries, except for some brief intervals, the capital of
Khmer kings was Yasodharapura, northwest of Tonle Sap
Lake, on the right bank of the Siem Reap River. Today,
this place is called Angkor Thom. One mile south of this
Great Capital, King Suryavarman II (1114 to 1163) decided to build the perfect reproduction of the macrocosm.
This was to be Angkor Wat, the culmination of all architectural and artistic efforts of the previous centuries. With
the privilege of hindsight, we today can now see that the
elaborate building of Angkor—Capital and Temple—was
the three-hundred-year-long preparation of a suitable stage
on which the smile of Angkor could briefly flower under
the intuitive tutelage of the second Khmer genius, Jayavarman VII.

Jayavarman VII's revolutionary change can best be appreciated today in the Bayon building which he constructed at Angkor Thom. The Bayon, standing at the
exact center of the Capital—as Mount Meru at the exact
center of the macrocosm—dwarfed every other building.
It was a pyramidlike structure, 175 yards long and 153
yards wide, with fifty-four stone towers. As one interlocking mass of towers, terraces, halls, and corridors, it rose
140 feet high. It was divided into eight sections, had four
chapels and 1520 yards of intricate inner and outer corridoring. The inside walls carved in relief depicted scenes
from Khmer history, the daily life of each section of the
people, celestial dancers (*apsaras*), and the divine guardians

of the Temple. Outside on each side of the main tower there looks down at you the still vigorous symbol of Jayavarman's achievement: a colossal head of the smiling king represented as the Lord Buddha exulting in the joy of his people at the blessedness of their being human. Such an image with such a motif has not emerged in any other place at any other time throughout the 6000 years of known Asian history.

In this Buddha face was expressed Jayavarman VII's simple but far-reaching change: instead of the aniconic *lingam*, faceless, blank, nonhuman in appearance, symbol merely of passion and strength and masculinity—as well as of love and gentleness, he substituted a statue of the Lord Buddha. In it were personalized the passion, the love, and the gentleness. And, according to the ancient Khmer rite, Jayavarman VII identified himself with this statue by conferring on it a new double name—his own and Buddha's.

This was the new image of the cosmic man, the heavenly adoptee, the divinized mortal. To cap all this, he opened the eyes of the Buddha face into a glance. And he opened its lips, not into a hopeless exhaling of all self and all existence, but in a genuinely human smile.

That smiling face of Angkor shone until the jungle tendrils closed in around the glory of Angkor in the last decades of the fifteenth century. In making this innovation, Jayavarman VII was following some personal intuition; but he was able to catapult this intuition into the concrete reality of national daily life because of three hundred years of evolution. Between the death of Jayavarman II in 854 and his own accession in 1191, the religious texture of the Khmer mind had changed. The Khmers had progressed far beyond the crude Brahmanic adaptation made by Jayavarman II in the ninth century.

It was no longer merely the king who could be identified with the god—and thus be participant in the god's immunity from death and insignificance. A tradition had grown up among the ordinary people producing a cohesion from the lowliest workman to the King's right-hand men: to be associated with the cult of Angkor meant happiness in this life and immortality in the next—even if you merely carved a lintel, carried paving stones, polished the woodwork, or cleaned out the royal stables. For, in popular belief, Angkor was the center of the earth. And, being a faithful copy of the heavenly Mount Meru, it was the abode of the universe's Lord and his divinized followers.

The teachings of Buddha in the Theravada (the stricter form) were introduced into Cambodia somewhere around the second century A.D. Well before the tenth century, Mahayana (the more liberal) Buddhism gained some foothold. But it was the personal intuition of Jayavarman VII that made the difference. Had he a personal experience of his own? Was it merely a powerful instinct for synchresis? Did a little-known strain of Buddhism, a very faithful tradition dating from the Buddha himself, transplant itself to Cambodia and flower under Jayavarman VII? We will never know. We do know that Jayavarman VII's innovation is so isolated in the history of Buddhism and of Asia that nothing ordinary will explain it.

When Jayavarman established Buddhism as the official religion in Cambodia, he chose as its permanent ikon the smile, the smiling face of the Buddha. He made that smile and all its deep connotation the symbol and witness of value—personal value and national value. He thus transformed the daily life of Khmer men and women and children, molded their architecture, inspired their political ideals, nourished a personal piety and a community sentiment, swallowed their time and energies, and gave them a wellspring for their interest in life.

In his choice of symbol he was faithful to an ancient

tradition. For, significantly, the central trait of Buddha in the memory of his followers throughout Asia was always his smile. We find in the earliest writings following Siddhartha's death the most beautiful rationale of the smile as a characteristic of a human being and of Siddhartha's smile in particular. That smile, apparently, during his lifetime was a mirror of the compassion which had been shown him by the divine. It was compassion not for a pitiful emptiness in him, nor for a worthless misery in him. It was rather the complacent joy of the divine delighted at the harmonious beauty and the tranquillity of ordered elements which resulted from the union of the divine and the human. For thus the divine had measured itself to suit a human capacity. But in filling that capacity, it made what was human more than human, quieting all febrile needfulness, enriching all poverty of will.

After Siddhartha's death, however, there was a gap of more than four hundred years before sculptors and artists could bring themselves to portray him. There was a reason for this: all his life, he had preached against appearance for appearance's sake; and, to judge from the impact he had, the effect of his inner power must have been so telling that all his followers concluded that it was impossible to transmit this power in visible images. Besides, dying he had been received into the undying and the invisible. He was no longer trapped in the "component parts" he had declared on his deathbed to be the source of our corruption. To what purpose, then, portray those "component parts"? So they cast the Buddha only in symbols: a footprint, an empty throne, a lotus flower, a wheel.

When the first heads of Buddha appeared at the beginning of the Christian era, they were fashioned under the direct influence of classical Greek models. These first busts of Siddhartha are stylized, conforming rigidly to a set pattern of thirty-two characteristics, the "marks of a great man" (the finial on top of the head, a mole between the eyebrows—the third eye of enlightenment, elongated earlobes, symbolic positions of hands and feet, cropped hair, to mention a few); each of them had a tribal, ethnic, cultural, or local origin in India which scholars have traced. But put together they did not image forth a person, rather, a construct of idealized parts. The focal point, however, of this idealized Buddha face was always and still is the smile—quiet, emptied, and emptying. Unevocative and unresponding. And what strikes us is the yawning difference between that Buddha smile and the smile on the face of Buddha at Angkor Wat: quiet, too, this latter, but fully active, totally filled, ringing with a self-filled joy, evocative and responsive in a human reply to every human face that looks upon it.

Difficult as it may be for the Western mind to grasp the difference in those two Buddha smiles, we do have a parallel in our own tradition of the West where we can look to clarify the deep significance which underlies the difference.

The *Hermes* of Praxiteles (fourth century B.C.) has the face of Greek antiquity and the smile of an ancient ethos: man's single-handed struggle with fates that are always stronger than he, will always outlast him, but sometimes give him a few years' respite before closing in on him as their carrion. Upon him is conferred no worth beyond the struggle, no accomplishment beyond desire. The smile of *Hermes* reflects no cosmic paradigm of the self. What makes him smile is neither compassion nor being compassionated. The curve of the mouth is not softened by love. Laughter and humor were evoked by misfortune of others, pratfalls of humankind which one was lucky enough to escape—for the moment. Each man's face was negligible, unloving; and, in that fate, he ceased finally to be human. The brow of *Hermes* is smooth and flawless. The eyes are open, but blank and soulless, lit by no vision. The smile is close lipped, narrow, at once self-satisfying and self-pitying, looking for no human answer for itself from another. The lips seem gripped at the corners by a tinge of vacuous regret. The *Hermes* says: "I am beautiful. As beautiful as a mortal face alone can be. And I am dust and will return to dust and nothingness."

Over 1700 years later, the face of the West had been changed, molded again from the soul outward by the deep meaning and effect of Christianity. Western man accepted a new paradigm: all things human were the gift and legacy of a saving god to every man and woman. Love was now more than mere excitement. Laughter and smiles touched a cosmic chord beyond mere amusement. The *Smiling Angel* of Rheims (thirteenth century A.D.) looks out upon us with a mischievous and radiant expression of greeting and response. Hovering in the subtle eye rims and playing hide-and-seek in the smile lines which weave eyes and nostrils and mouth and chin into a happy wreath of expression, is a whole portrait of human salutation, unmistakable and requiring human response from every human viewer. With that smile, the *Angel* testifies that God himself laughs at each new dawn and at every wry turn of human behavior. Love and compassion flow over the fabric of febrile humor and brittle glee, making a new and different cloth in which our human expression is draped and deeply warmed. From a ground of hope and pride in the self, the *Angel* is listening to a human harmony, looking out with and upon the vision of human dignity and eternal security announced by the followers of Jesus and expressed in the shooting spires and grandiose confidence of the Gothic cathedral.

Between the *Hermes* and the *Angel* a transforming vision had touched the human soul; and all that was portrayed in its name bore its unmistakable stamp. Between the first carved heads of Buddha from the second to the fourth centuries and the Buddha heads of Angkor Wat in the twelfth century, some similarly transforming vision must have shone.

Astoundingly enough the *Gandhara* Budda (fourth century A.D.) may have been the model for the *Smiling Angel* fashioned eight hundred years later. If that is so, it is dramatic testimony to the infinity of difference wrought by the touch of spirit in human things. Both heads are almost feminine in cast. Both are inclined, as if listening to a conversation. Both have oval faces. Both are smiling—each in its own way. As the *Angel* is listening to human harmony, the *Gandhara* Buddha is listening to silence. The latter's traits make up a litany of human emptiness. Lacking that warmth without which no one can feel the hand of pity or know compassion. Unmerciful, because proffering no salvation which every object of mercy deserves. Unrecognizing, because here the smile greets you with *Ta Twam Asi* ("Thou Art Thou"); and, in all moments of recognition, it is an "I" which greets a "Thou." Not even enigmatic, for it holds within its expression no secret for man to discover. It does not say "I am"—like Michelangelo's God touching the finger of Adam in the Sistine Chapel. Nor does it state "I am not"—mutely, like El Greco's *Count Orgaz*. It is expressionless fixity.

Wherever you go in the Garden of Buddha, outside Cambodia of the Khmers, the difficulty of response to that smile is an index of its quality. You may want to smile back with pleasure; but the Buddha's smile is willfully unremembering of pleasure. To smile in recognition, then; but the Buddha smiles as a shadow which may love you infinitely but cannot be drawn into the light of your knowledge. To smile with understanding, perhaps? But the eyes of the Buddha smile are unseeing and receive no message of understanding. Then, to smile merely as one

individual meeting another; but the Buddha never aban-
dons a man to the dark of the self. Perhaps you react in
the end with a puzzled and unechoing smile or one that
vanishes quickly. And thus it is all around Buddhism's
shrines and monuments—the seventy-two-foot statue of
Buddha at Taipei, the jade Buddha in the Tai mountains
near Shanghai, and any one of hundreds of thousands of
Buddha statues in all the city temples and wayside shrines
of Asia.

Until we come to Angkor Wat and the *Jayavarman Buddha* executed within a century of the *Smiling Angel* of
Rheims. It is this Buddha which fully and finally ex-
presses to us Siddhartha's message of humanness and the
meaning it derives from what is more than human. It also
indicates to us the brilliance of King Jayavarman VII's intuition of this message as the basis for the Angkor vision of
the Castle. Done in quadruplex, one on each side of a
square, monumental tower set up at Angkor, this Buddha
compels your response. It is crowned, not with the un-
earthly finial, but with tier upon tier of a colonnaded, intricately carved, and decorative tiara. A broad, full-lipped
smile wreathes and embellishes chin, mouth, nostrils,
eyes, and temples. The eyes are open and seeing and hu-
morous. They look at you; and the *Jayavarman Buddha*
laughs; and your human laugh can respond to it.

By some trompe l'oeil of sculpture, now it seems to be
laughing, now it seems to be chuckling, now it seems to be
merely smiling. Yet, it is colored with a compassion which
only human beings can give and only human beings can
receive. It is human, amused, amusing, awakening in the
onlooker a sense of welcome and surprise—as every genuinely human smile—and making one aware of the inner
dimension with which we constantly endeavor to humanize our pleasures, our pains, our birth, and our death. Between the fourth century when the *Gandhara* was executed

and the twelfth century when Jayavarman accomplished his designs, something happened among the Khmers which was as transforming and humanizing as the Roman vision of Jesus had been for Western man. Jayavarman knew not merely the facts about Siddhartha's life. Personally, he must have experienced the spirit. There must have been a *pati divina*, a touch of the Divine in his inner life illuminating the corners of his humanness and affording him a technique to translate it for his people into a tangible vision of the Castle.

The smile of Angkor remains as a constant and accurate symbol of that vision. For, to be sure, the smile was not all.

The Khmers, molded by Jayavarman's intuition and guided by his genius, accomplished much. They carved on stone and wood the new message: The self is valuable. The self is immortal. The self loves and is loved. Not merely at Angkor but throughout Cambodia, they used the only mass media at their disposal: temple walls, statues, frescoes, carvings, buildings, popular music, national festivals. Always it was the same assertion: that the Khmers were identified with the smiling Buddha-King, were already transformed and divinized in this life, and that Heaven—Mount Meru—was among them.

As Jayavarman and his people acquired by conquest of arms the whole of Vietnam, Burma, Thailand, Malay, Laos, and a portion of Sumatra, all of this became the Empire of the Smile. His kingdom was interlaced with royal roads, tracks for caravans, and intricate canals for barges. Rice production was trebled by irrigation canals. He dotted the plains with artificial lakes plentiful in fish. Industries allied to the building fever of the Khmers sprang up in stone, metal, woodwork, weaving, perfumery, pottery; cuisine, pharmacy, home, school, all benefited from the efflorescence of energy.

He constructed 121 hostels for the pilgrims who came from all over his empire. He built 102 hospitals for the sick under the auspices of Buddha the Healer, *Bhaishajyaguru Vaiduryaprabha*, "The Master of Remedies with the Shining Beryl." We even know the annual food consumption of his hospital system: 11,192 tons of rice; 2124 kilos of sesame seeds; 105 kilos of cardamom; 3402 nutmegs; 1960 boxes of salve for blisters, sores, and hemorrhoids. Each hospital had two doctors, two storekeepers, two nurses, and fourteen attendants. "The sufferings of the people constitute the suffering of the King, more than his own sufferings do"—run the words of one of Jayavarman's inscriptions.

All of this happened here, where the self came alive again; where interest flourished, and men and women cared. Here, apparently, they were rescued from systems and formulae of the Eightfold Path by an intuition of human encounter with spirit and by a recognition of the self and of spirit as real forever. Here they listened anew for the laughter of the self and heard its beauty speak.

Neither in Brahmanism nor in Buddhism of the traditional kind was that self ever vindicated. In the former, man was a stranger in an alien world fashioned by impersonal forces and fated like himself to go back into the same sun. In the latter, the self was to be fled, discarded like a hindering coat of iron. Jayavarman's innovation: the inner "self" of a man is made valuable and immortal by association with the divinity during this life and for eternity. We find in the art and accomplishments at Angkor that their creators eliminated all the elements we find in India, in Burma, in Sumatra, and elsewhere, which degraded that inner self. They substituted a terraced style of building, corniced and fluted and chiseled with delicate forms, for the awesome chunks of sacrificial houses and moaning temples to be found elsewhere. It all embodied the divinization of the world by the Divine and consequently the human value for all things in the human world.

Absent from their plastic arts at Angkor is any trace of those erotic and macabre scenes which vilify much of Indian art in our eyes. They abolished the typical *hanchement* of Indian figures (weight on one foot; opposite hip emphasized) together with the impersonal vacuity of the face. At Angkor, human forms stand strong and straight smiling out at life. No tortured convolution of human limbs. No wallowing copulation of half-human deities or multi-headed devils ravishing submissive women. The huge bronze sleeping Vishnu of the eleventh century is a happy man sleeping the sleep of the just, not Vishnu in one or other of his interminably wearisome incarnations, and not as a mortal caught in the hands of impersonal death and unconscious Nirvana. Lokeshvara, the Compassionate, laughs as a man. And Prajnapuramita, the Perfection of Wisdom, smiles approvingly at human ingenuity.

Walls, pillars, ceilings, doorways, floors, all proliferate with vegetal designs, flowering garlands, and foliate motifs. Rainbow-shaped lintels curve with colors and convex medallions. Statues wear the Smile and gesture with their hands benignly. They are draped in hieratical styles and poses, decorated with jewels and diadems; flesh and musculature are rendered impressionistically. Even supernatural figures were humanized: the Naga serpent had a human head; the Hamsa geese had smiling eyes; the Garuda birds were joyous caryatids.

Here at Angkor, no temple is a mausoleum. No tower is a funerary monument. For the Wheel of Existence with its ennui of endlessness had been broken with the Smile. Every tomb is a house for venerating the mortals made immortal by the adoptive love of the Lord Buddha and the Lord of the Universe. Streets, halls, temples, and houses throng with statues, each one representing the deceased—

but not as dead. These were new architectural bodies, surrogates for the deceased now become cosmic and heavenly. Even the poorest have little figurines for the same purpose. In the renewed sense of self, redeemed by the more than human, all is freshly human; and what is not of itself human has been humanized.

You may be in awe at the physical dimensions of Angkor and marvel at its durability. But you are not solemn with reverential fear. Rather, enlivened with a smile of expectancy. For the Khmer principle of art was simple: it was not for religious instruction primarily, nor to commemorate royal glories; but, pleasingly, to materialize the divine in human terms.

You realize then that Angkor was a fitting stage for the celebration of the Day of the Smile. You can almost see the Khmers as they celebrated around the palace at Angkor Thom: acrobats walking on tightropes between the twelve towers of Prasat Suor Prat; tumblers flying ecstatically around the Terrace of the Elephants; choruses of girls dancing before the King's Gate; singers enlivening everybody's ears with quick tunes and popular songs; performing monkeys swinging wildly on ribboned poles, chattering all the while; parakeets, cockatoos, cardinal birds crooning and cackling; food tents open; the people breakfasting within the smile of a new day and a fresh year. In the golden light of the morning, the Bayon and the palace and the tower temples shimmer with polished grays, old yellows, purples, sandstone reds, and brown tinting. All in Angkor Thom and all in Angkor Wat seem to be mirrors of that wonderful smile of Angkor shining from the height of the Bayon and saying that it was good to be alive, good to be human, because the human had been compassionated by the divine, and even the whimsical laughter of men and women had become a sacral feature of mankind and mankind's daily living.

The end of it all at Angkor came relatively swiftly in the fourteenth and fifteenth centuries. The Thais attacked from the northwest, the Laotians from the northeast, the Vietnamese and Chams—traditional enemies of the Khmer—from the east and the south. All thirsted for blood and loot and vengeance on their erstwhile superiors. They were aided by the superpower of the day, the Mongols, who themselves invaded the land of the Khmers. Internally, the Khmers had weakened. Mass conscription for continually sustained public works, unsuccessful foreign wars, harassment by guerrilla forces making forays across the plain toward Tonle Sap, intentional reduction of the population, ossification of the central power at Angkor, all these made the Khmer empire an easy prey.

But, most profoundly, there was a religious change. Singhalese Buddhist missionaries flooded the country in the late thirteenth and early fourteenth centuries. They preached against the Religion of the Smile, and inculcated strict Buddhism (Theravada), tearing at the human beauty of Angkor like ravening wolves, declaring its visible accomplishments a blasphemy and a degradation of the truth. Slowly they made headway; and the classical doctrines of personal passivity, anti-material outlook, abhorrence of all personal cult took root. Veneration by king and commoner waned. Faith in the divinization of the human disappeared as Theravada Buddhism spread and the sociopolitical framework crumbled.

Shorn of its northern, eastern, and western buffer territories, stripped of its fleets, defeated in open battle, its towns looted, its canals disrupted, within a short time Cambodia was reduced to a mere rump of its former self. At the opening of the fifteenth century, under repeated attacks, the court moved from Angkor to Phnom Penh. And Angkor was left naked and unprotected against the waiting fingers of the jungle which now closed in around it, as Theravada Buddhism closed around the Khmer soul. And the all-pervading listlessness of the Garden of Buddha crept back once more over Cambodia, dimming Khmer humor with enigmatic heaviness. The Smile was gone. With the vision.

Trampled successively by Mongols, Chinese, Burmese, Portuguese, Spanish, and French, Cambodia emerged after World War II as a kingdom. Since then it has lost its king and become a pawn in the Southeast Asian conflict. Angkor has been used by North Vietnamese regulars and Vietcong insurgents as a wayside station. The roar of B-52 bombers, the sonic boom of jet fighters, the scream of mortar and shell, and the hail of automatic weapons' fire have all shaken its walls. The Khmers have been used as guerrillas by Communists, Vietnamese, and by the CIA. Many of them are refugees. Many live on mercenary money. Proud memory of their former empire is as faint for them as Ottoman glories are for Kurdistan Turks—a matter of myth and a source for popular fabling.

Cambodia together with the whole of South Asia is being leavened today by Western technology and ways of living. Against that, Buddhism cannot even compete. In the Garden of Buddha, there are more than thirty-five nations, over three hundred languages and dialects, some seventeen million square miles through which almost 7000 years of known history have swept. Today, three hundred million Buddhists worship at two million shrines cared for by 800,000 monks and nuns. It subsists in retirement. But, under pain of self-liquidation, Buddhism cannot afford to come out and adopt the ways of the foreigner. And there is no evidence that the Khmer vision of the Castle can ever flourish again, even in a modern form. It was possible at one time, in one place, and within the historical conditions of one people. But human events have banished the Smile of Angkor forever.

Today, when you walk around the willow meadows of
Tonle Sap and through the silent pine woods, the five
towers and the upper stories of Angkor Wat peer out just
above the jungle top. The traceries of its buildings appear
as aery strokes of an infinitely light hand that once etched
a human beauty with marvelous whimsy beneath the
overlooking mountains, between the thin horizon line and
the clouds of the sky. Sometimes, when the afternoon
heat has been dissipated, you will see a pair of young
lovers wandering among the ruins. All is quiet beneath the
moon: Angkor Wat seems to be a great house whose inhabitants are merely sleeping securely until some morning
time of joy. But in Phnom Penh and Sihanoukville, and in
Bangkok of Thailand as in Singapore and throughout
Asia, Buddhists are learning Western languages and sciences. And their new-found knowledge will not lead them
back to the Smile that once embellished this area.

Sometimes at dawn, when the sun breaks over the
Great Temple, an illusion of eternity seizes your eyes.
The worn, shaggy look fades for a few instants from Angkor Wat. And those five towers with their terraces and
gardens and shattered corridors come alive in a peculiar
way. They do not hang over against the sky and the earth
like the Pharaoh's tomb by the Nile. They become
rather an ecto-form of fancied escape from the cloddish solidity of the ground and from the grinning inevitability of
each day's ennui, from the earth which awaits the entry of
each mortal thing into its capacious folds. The Khmers,
the Byzantines of South Asia, somehow or other traced in
ageless stone that moment-long thrill of exultation which
fathers every human smile and makes every human laugh,
a gesture of absolute independence from the evil of banality.

Sometimes on the eve of the full moon, old women
from the surrounding villages come on foot to the Bayon.

Shrunken and wispy in stature, smiling toothlessly, they stand in front of the Smiling Buddha. And Jayavarman, their most glorious ancestor, laughs down to greet them. In their day-to-day lives, to be human is once again to be worthless; to be woman is fatal; each leaf that falls is a personal tragedy; the passing of each year seems like a fading of their own vital powers. Here, however, while their incense sticks burn, they pray. Not that their sons may return from the terrible war, and not that their daughters may bear a son—to have a son nowadays means to have one more grave to tend. But that they will find the Smile in eternity. When you draw near and look into their eyes, what you see hushes your mind with a sudden feeling that you have never understood anything; there are always tears in their answering smile of hope.

8

WITTENBERG
Dignity of Reason

The Wittenberg vision of the human Castle was like no other vision in human history.

Moses on Sinai, Jesus on his Cross, Mohammed in his Hegira, Buddha beneath the Bo Tree, Constantine gazing at a sign in the sky—all appear as transfigured by the invisible, the ineffable, filtering through the chinks of their mortality. Thereby they inflamed men and women to set out and give their Castle vision substance and validity in the visible surroundings of their ordinary lives. Nothing of this kind marks the Wittenberg vision.

Even by such a simple measure, it stands apart. Without any single divine outbreak, any one singular experience of the "beyond," it might seem at first glance to have been the product of a vast human mechanism rather than the inspiration of the invisible: a *deus ex machina* resulting from an assemblage of men and women and the extraordinary efforts of their wills, intellects, ideals, virtues, pains, prejudices, vices, and triumphs. Yet, clearly, like all human visions of the Castle, it was of capital consequence.

Unlike others, this Castle vision arose within one of the most violent revolts we know of in the history of spirit among men. Above the clamor of shibboleths and slogans that flew fast and thick between lusty antagonists; and through the plague of papers—writs, bulls, proclamations, confessions, disputations, books, and pamphlets—which blanketed Europe and marked the birth and building of this vision between 1517 and 1700, there cried the voice of a deep yearning frustrated in its very fibers and seeking some egress for itself. In this yearning were planted the seeds, and from them grew the essence of the Wittenberg vision.

The yearning was ancient in its instincts. Its roots can be traced back to the fourth century A.D. when Europeans realized that a new public force had arrived in their midst; that it had done so in utter silence without clangor or flashing triumphs; and that nothing they could do would undo the Christian beliefs which had, by that time, pervaded all. On the contrary, these beliefs were irresistible in the dying fires of the Roman Empire. In our factual modern minds, the tendency is to *think* and to *express* this happening in quantitative terms: so many single items of belief; so many festivals; so many millions of Christians versus so many pagans; so many churches, monasteries, schools, prominent men; and much of the like. Thus, we miss the essential. We take poll counts, as if numbers explained the force of choice in human affairs. We reckon physical forces, as if these explained why men and women act, or why they become what they become.

In the world of the fourth century, there was primarily an event of spirit: a dimension of faith, a love of the eternal and permanent, and a dream of its perfection as being the lot and the destiny of each person. Not just emotionalism and not just enthusiasm. It strongly nourished the latter; and it frequently broke out in the former; but it would not be reduced to either. Nor was it wholesale fantasy based on superstitions and myths fed into hungry minds. Fantasy and myth fare ill at the hands of hard facts; and that was a world of cruelly hard facts: wars, disease, decadence, social disruption, poverty, hunger, ruthlessness, and crime. The modern Ik people, described by Colin Turnbull, the population of Sekelia, and the myth-immersed peoples of India today show us what happens when human beings tussle merely with hard facts and with fantasy and myth as their only resources. They perish.

What arrived in the fourth century, and what echoed still and beckoned at the far horizon of the sixteenth-century vision, was a dimension of inner living. The ways and means in which people conducted their daily lives were conformed to an innerliness which mirrorlike flashed brightly with images, convictions, aspirations reflected from a vision not arising from the physical quanta of those daily lives and not the product of mind and imagination. But, of formless beauty and of timeless being, they transfused the spatial forms and time-bound factors of those daily lives. All was divinized in their eyes: because one individual man was divine, all individuals had access to divinity. People no longer sought reasons to convince themselves to believe, but only reasons to explain their belief. Reason and logic worked on belief as on a primary datum, not to approve or disapprove that belief, but only to understand it and illustrate it.

We today read of all this in their literature. We listen to their songs. We scrutinize their faces and gestures in frescoes, mosaics, statues, and ikons. We walk among the remains of what they built, reconstructing their minds and feelings and intents from what we feel and intuit. We find none of the self-contained satisfaction and soulless grace of classical Greece and Rome whose monuments are like concave mirrors which only reflect the shadow darkening our mortal days and the light we kindle to make our darkness bearable. But in nascent Christian civilization of that time, what we see is different: eyes and words have an ongoing vibrancy without tension; the look is exalted without any twist of hallucination; faces have a courage that has no brashness; gestures have a regnancy lacking imperiousness; the whole is calmed in awe. And strong. Persistently strong. Never crimped in fear. They appear as cohesive, well "put together," walking with a guarantee made personally to them: all the promises will be made good.

Such was the freshness of those fourth-century beginnings that threw rainbow lights across twelve centuries. Promises—clear, new, supremely attractive: "You shall be free to be human. Free of fear. Free of error. Free of all slavery in body and mind. Free of false beliefs. Free of anything transiently accurate but permanently inaccurate. Free of the human bondage. For your humanness has been exalted by the love of God who died for your sake." Augustine of Hippo, with his epigrammatic Latin, fashioned a motto for the new human being: *"Ama! Et fac quod vis!"* (Love! Then do what you will!). It was to the tune of this springtime promise and men's wish for its prize that whole populations in Europe, Africa, and the Near East had turned into fervent Christians by the end of the sixth century A.D.

Historically, that promise was only partially fulfilled. For Christianity never solved social ills such as slavery and the substatus of women, nor political ills such as tyranny and totalitarianism, nor the mental problems which freedom and responsibility pose. The yearning, therefore, went underground, frustrated. Within two hundred years, by the eighth century, the Christian church as educator of Europeans and holder of the promise came into the hands of political clerics and clerical politicians. From the time that Pope Leo III scurried off to Paderborn in 799 for help from Charlemagne, the Church, led by Gregory VII in the ninth century, and by Innocent III and Innocent IV in the twelfth century, pursued a consistent search for political, economic, and cultural domination.

The yearning was further exacerbated when, from the eleventh century onward, European minds were trained by reasoning ecclesiastics. In the 1100s and 1200s they initiated men into the dignity and the power of human reason. But it was all very clumsy: they made the acceptability of belief and of the divine depend on the force of a syllogism and the reasoning of a theological argument. God was accessible because of a logical premise; his mysteries were contained in Latin terminology.

And, clearly, the seating of reason as supreme arbiter in an already completely political church, was as explosive as gunpowder thrown on an open fire. Politics and reason were adopted by churchmen as the bulwark of their Christianity; but they forbade its use except at their own bidding. They built a vast machine, but insisted it serve only their own interests. It was fatal.

When Europeans started moving out to examine their physical universe by exploration and scientific means, when the humanism of the fifteenth and sixteenth centuries gave them back a voice and a sense of self that had been lacking for centuries, the yearning for fulfillment of the ancient promise emerged again. Not as a sudden departure, not as a revolt from normalcy, not as an unseemly and unpredictable break in the perfect harmony. On the contrary. In an age which produced such earth-shaking giants as Copernicus, Galileo, Michelangelo, and Columbus, the Wittenberg revolt was as logical and inevitable as the end product of any machine.

With such a general seething background as seedbed, the six centuries preceding the outbreak of the Wittenberg vision came to be marked by a halting progression which, now looking backward, we can see clearly prepared the clamor for reason and freedom of conscience heard in the sixteenth century. Thomas Aquinas wrote Greek logic with biblical faith, emphasizing the supremacy of personal conscience and exalting reason. (St. Bonaventure, far seeing, called Thomas "father of all the heretics," the one who taught men "to reason their way out of faith." And Stephen Tempier, Bishop of Paris, burned Aquinas' writings in 1272 because "their rationalism made faith impossible." Abelard, Socrates of the Gauls, described all the mysteries of faith as only problems to be solved by logic, until he came up against the one mystery his logic could never solve: the power of his own passion. Thomas à. Kempis and Dante Alighieri in the fourteenth century protested; one pleaded for a renewal of life in the spirit of Jesus and renouncement of power politics; the other urged a separation of church and state. John (Dr. Wicked-Believe) Wycliffe, Oxford don, sent out his "Lollards" to read the Bible to the common people and challenged the absolute authority of churchmen; (his bones were exhumed after death to be burned and thrown into the river Swift, "to wipe oute his unsavourie memorie.") Girolamo Savonarola cried to his fellow Florentines: "Listen to me! You are sitting by the rivers of sin," rejected Pope Alexander VI's offer of a cardinal's hat ("I want a hat full of blood, not a blood-red hat"), and was tortured, hanged, and finally burned in 1498 for advocating a civil government. The Czech John Hus was burned at the stake in 1415 for rebelling against his bishop; and he whispered through the flames: "Now you burn a goose [Hus = goose], but in a century, you will have a swan which you can neither boil nor burn." Indeed, finally, it was the swan: Martin Luther.

But clear as its antecedents may have been, the Wittenberg vision of the human Castle can be most confusing as we move away from those antecedents to the moment of the vision itself. Its origin—not in a transfiguring experience, but in a feeling of a lack, a sense of what might or should have been glimpsed in rainbow light from prisms dimming but not yet lost—this was the origin that determined its experimenting, searching, and very voluble character. Its assemblage of impressive personalities, interlocking clashes, and crisscrossing fissures begin to develop in kaleidoscopic dimensions. On still another level one may be confused by the wholly theological appearance of Wittenberg—as though it might be altering the world on the basis of a sectarian religious squabble, rather than in a response to a shining light of the spirit.

And on the most pragmatic level, looking with a purely historical eye at the chaotic abuse and the reigning circumstances, so banal, almost comic in their tragedy, that reached fever pitch in the 1500s, the temptation is to throw up one's hands and parody the cynical illogicality of Voltaire and observe that if Luther had not existed, he would have had to be invented. It was bizarre. There was a traveling salesman: Johann Tetzel of Leipzig, Dominican priest, theologian, doctor, professor. His director: Pope Leo X, who devised a new sales campaign to get funds for refurbishing St. Peter's Basilica in Rome. His wares: indulgences. His prices: exact monetary value for the forgiveness of every imaginable sin of the already dead. His sales technique: a cardinal red booth, a receipt box, and a marvelous gift for mimicking the pleas of the dead who suffered in Purgatory and craved the monetary help of the living so that they might escape the punishment of fire. His sales pitch: a memorable jingle ("As soon as the coin in the coffer rings, The soul from Purgatory springs.")

Tetzel set up shop near Wittenberg in October of 1517. By the last week of the month, the young university professor of Bible studies, Martin Luther, had heard all about Tetzel, witnessed his act, and returned, incensed, to his cell (he was an Augustinian friar). He started writing out in Latin all his objections to the politics and the reason of his Church as exemplified in Tetzel and his mission.

On October 31, 1517, Eve of All Saints (and here no one knows if we have myth or historical fact), Luther stood outside the oaken doors of Wittenberg Castle church and nailed a copy of his objections, his "Ninety-five Theses," to the right-hand panel. Quickly Saxon printers translated them into vernacular German and circulated them handily throughout the German states. The act catapulted Luther to leadership in the Reform. "The Candle of Reformation is lighted," exclaimed the Reformers depicted in an early Protestant lithograph which shows a puffing pope, a water-sprinkling friar, and the devil disguised as a dog, all three moaning: "We cannot put it out!" And although, like Albrecht Dürer's *Four Horsemen of the Apocalypse*, most of the visionaries did not know *where* they were going, they were at least going.

Tetzel, a simple man, retired in tears and perpetual melancholy to a monastery, blamed himself for the subsequent brouhaha, and ultimately died in seclusion. Luther wrote to him consolingly: "Don't take it so hard, my brother. You didn't start the racket. This child had another father."

Yet for all the embroilment that surrounded it, at this moment of initial exaltation we can perceive the lasting beauty, the permanent desirability of the Wittenberg vision. The abuses had been tragically real. The instincts of the Reformers were genuine; their cry was sincere:

> If we can only free ourselves of the manacles on our reason! If we can only free ourselves from this cumbrous machine! If we can only get back to the primitive truth and purity of the Gospel: to Jesus on the Mount, and

away from the merciless Christ of infallible theologians with their strictures, their excommunications, their whips, their torture and fire and sword; to the loving God of the Fourth Gospel, and away from the *Deus Trinus* of caviling philosophers; to the free adoration of our common Father in the fellowship of the Cup of Love and away from those Latinate bowings and payments and hocus-pocus; to the liberty of God's beloved children, and away from being pawns of power-mad papists; to the pure aid of our consciences made righteous by true belief, and away from the cringing dependencies on the arbitrary wave of a human hand to absolve us from sins—mortal, venial, formal, material, ecclesiastical, canonical, *de jure* and *de facto*—all remitted, dispensed, indulgenced according to the loveless minds of bureaucrats and the base imaginings of jealous celibates. If only there can be pure love of Jesus, of his Church, of all men, then we will be God's saints, the Elect of Jesus, true citizens, satisfied human beings.

What is there in common between Jesus, the Lord of Gentle Love and Salvation, and a pope buckling on his sword for battle [Julius II had done just that scant years before Luther's revolt], prince-bishops who indulge in every human vice, children from noble families consecrated cardinals at the age of 7, fattened monks, contemptuous scholar-priests and thieving friars? Would Jesus sign a treaty with Venice or the Holy Roman Emperor? Would he send out armed henchmen to collect tribute from vassals? Would he have vassals? Would he rule by fear? Would he deny us knowledge and freedom to learn?

It was the ancient yearning, a harkening back to the *Ama! Et fac quod vis!* of Augustine. It was a glimpse of the hoary promise shimmering through a random chink in the gray clouds of the traditional day: that Jesus would bring immunity from error; that he guaranteed a beauty in being human; that he underwrote the terrible weakness of all human mortality; that he alone was man's ruler; that he had purified human reason so that it would not err; and that, with this reason, man had an open door into knowledge of spirit, of goodness, and of God himself.

There was reborn, then, a strain of that mysticism which had originally come to the West from Palestine and has never quite disappeared, particularly from among Protestants. It was a faith prior to all reasoning, a belief prior to all logic. It was acceptance of the divine without any prior "because"—other than the presence of the divine which then embellished all reasoning and ennobled all rationality. It was the naked conviction that the divine had become immediately accessible to humans, bringing about purposiveness in belief, idealism in hope, strength in love, and a sense of personal worth, of enthusiasm for being human.

At the outset, therefore, the very complexities that gave it birth also swiftly gave the Wittenberg vision very definite contours. It entailed a freeing of men's social and political and personal lives from clerical control: a freeing of their reason from church censorship, a freeing of their souls from imposed superstitions and the perpetuated childishnesses of ecclesiastical protectionism. It identified this heady liberation as the gateway to achieving the true dignity and beauty of men and women, a condition of living in which the natural power of human reason and the innate goodness of the individual conscience would enable a person to reach happiness freely without threatening constraints, *because of a prior and established condition of human beings:* the divine presence and divinization of all things human. It was the ancient mysticism striving to free itself from the encrustations layered on it by clerical politics and the mental gymnastics of philosophers and theologians. All men would be priests in the Kingdom; human love would be ennobled; the promise of Jesus—Rock of Ages— would come about. Now they would journey to the new Jerusalem; and, in the sweet bye-and-bye, meet on that heavenly shore and exchange the Old Rugged Cross for a crown:

> O! Beulah Land, Sweet Beulah Land!
> As on the highest mount I stand,
> I look away across the sea,
> Where mansions are prepared for me!

Sometimes in almost parallel language, sometimes in equivalent terms, those early men of the Wittenberg vision anticipated the later aspirations of the eighteenth- and nineteenth-century romantics: leave human beings alone and free, saved from wrath and made pure, to walk the deep meadows of their living God's universe with reason as their shining guide until they reach the golden shores where amber treasures, fragrant with the sacred foam of Christ's flood tide mercy, are stored for their spirits' sustenance.

No one can doubt that this was the burning core of the Wittenberg vision. It is one of the biggest *ifs* in history to speculate what would have happened had it remained the central and dominating motive for Wittenberg. It did not—and for very tangible and understandable reasons; but it survived as a constantly recurring force in Protestantism right down into the last decades of the twentieth century, reappearing in the constant fragmentation and atomization, in the amazing pullulation of sects and groups that has characterized Protestantism almost from the beginning.

What came to the fore, instead, among Protestants was something else: the primacy of reason and the privilege of dissent. The causes are obvious. Something more deeply human was stirring their contemporaries than churchmen of that time ever permitted themselves to dream: the physical world was just beginning in a new way to exercise its fascination on men of their time—its beauty, its natural secrets, its undreamt-of extent and variety, its generosity, all beckoned to a perfection of human living never before perceived as possible or preached by the Church as the destined lot of human beings.

Against that background, the ideal of freedom to be human, to be unfettered in reason, to exercise dissent as a privilege of humanness, and thus to teach, to explore, to attempt, to think the supposedly unthinkable, burst out in full splendor. Within seventy years, clerics for whom Tetzel would surely serve as a badly tarnished and all too apt symbol were manifestly seen as enemies of the truth about the physical world.

Dissenting reason was enthroned as the chief expression of the ancient mysticism, the working of an individual's mind as his highest privilege in the kingdom of Jesus, precisely at the moment when ever-widening horizons in man's world poured oceans of new facts for his mind and teemed with new stimuli for his natural curiosity. Dissenting reason was so prized that it not only dethroned the clerics but was itself made immune from any restraint.

Even when it proceeded to pick away at the core of belief, reason was still exalted. The faith, in whose name reason was prized, was subject to its strictures. All the violence of the Reform was channeled into a vindication of reason—men's reason—as the principal means at their disposal to complete their humanness at a time when a definitive break had come in the one-thousand-year-old tradition of politics and social consciousness: nationalism as distinct from dynasty was born; self government, as distinct from feudal identity, became the ideal; the old medieval world was over and done with.

Again, unlike any of its predecessors, the practical circumstances of the Wittenberg vision took hold too quickly for its followers to catch their breath; too quickly to mature, to ripen in reflective spirits of a quiet age, and then move outward, first slowly and later in quickening waves. It was the headline happening of its day. It would ripen quickly or be swamped in the storm of its own making. It would perforce simultaneously mold and be molded. What started off as a religious event entertained primarily by theologians and philosophers—all with religious motives— became the direct antecedent to all we are today; it made possible the present condition of our civilization. What originated in a startling evocation of a millenniar faith made England, Germany, and the United States possible; it made science feasible and technotronic man an inevitability.

As if to set the Wittenberg vision in yet greater contrast, Luther himself mirrored more the temper of his times than the contours of any previous vision bearer. He was a big, powerfully built man with small piercing eyes, heavy jowls, curly hair, large belly, an extensive jaw, and expressive mouth; quick tempered, coarse in language; obstinate as a mule ("I will not recant," he stated flatly to the Emperor's face); at times beset by scruples and doubts, and at times exercising total personal infallibility ("Sin strongly!" he told Melanchthon "Believe more strongly!"); a firm believer in gnomes and elves and his personal encounters with Satan himself; a confirmed and vituperative anti-Semite; a marvelous popular preacher, a magic translator of the Bible; and, by his own philosophy, only a cog which would soon be followed and surrounded by greater and lesser cogs.

As counsel to his followers, Luther told them to "smite, slay and stab, secretly and openly" all who rebelled against him. Slaying and stabbing were standard. Everybody persecuted somebody. Some, such as the Anabaptists, were persecuted by everybody. The St. Bartholmew Day Massacre of August 24, 1572, accounted for at least 10,000 Protestants. The Thirty Years' War killed half the population of Germany, left about two and one-half million homeless with their cities, towns, hamlets, and villages in blood-grappled shreds, and included wholesale rape, burning, murder, destruction, and torture, with cannibalism in Pomerania and ritual crucifixion in the German Palatinate. The Catholic Inquisition did not outdo the Star Chamber in England or the "Iron Houses" of German and Scandinavian princes. Outwardly calm, confident, and pitilessly dedicated to their version of the truth, the participants on both sides acted no better than wild and witless beasts committing such crimes as leave us walleyed in horror today when we hear of their analogs in the Sudan, Nigeria, Pakistan, and Northern Ireland. Cruelty, sadism, killing, destruction—and, as a consequence, prejudice, fear, suspicion, hate, and ignorance—were the order of the day and the legacy of the Reform.

Such working out of the vision lacked any trace of the one vaunted trait of Christ's followers: gentle, patient, understanding love. In fact, it reproduced everything that the Reformers denounced, especially the dogmatism and mercilessness of the Romish Church. Quite logically, Russian Patriarch Komniakov reproached the visiting Archbishop of Canterbury in 1750: "All you Protestants are crypto-Papists!" Everybody on every side misbehaved in what must rank as the most disillusioning episode of Christianity's history. Hate and cruelty were permanent weapons in the hands of Protestants and their opponents alike. For Pope Leo X, Luther was a "scabby sheep," a "leper with a brain of brass and a nose of iron," "a drunken German." "Germany is the Pope's pig," gibed Luther, "so the Pope requires bacon and sausages from us," adding that "the only portion of the human anatomy the Pope has to leave uncontrolled is the hind end." Luther's more imaginative descriptions of pope, bishop, priest, monk, and nun embrace a truly amazing ambit of human obscenity.

It all had nothing whatever to do with a god of love.

With such strife and turmoil as midwife, and with a Pandora-like dictum that all men should follow the inclination of personal conscience and thus avoid answering to anyone, the twin hallmarks emerged which were to make this vision unique: the iron rule of individual and autonomous reason; and (as Sisyphus in theological garb) a constant flurry of dissents, divisions, and multiplication of churches, sects, and groups. There can be little wonder at the truly sparkling array of doctrines and differences that proliferated as Protestants multiplied in number and influence: Henry VIII of England, John Frederick of Saxony, Marguerite d'Angoulême, Jacob Arminius, Menno Simons, Philip Melanchthon, John Calvin, Theodore Beza, Hüldreich Zwingli, Thomas Münzer, John Knox, Tiny William Tyndale, Thomas Cranmer, John Wesley, Oliver Cromwell, and a host of others all exercising their recently liberated reason on the Bible and traditional beliefs. The result was once jeeringly described by Thomas Münzer as "Bible! Babel! Bubble!"

All seem to have been caught up in a centrifugal flow of events which each helped to create and foment, each one carving out a little fiefdom of dissent, all together throwing off a colorful bevy of followers bewildering in their professional dissonance: Anabaptists, Calvinists, Presbyterians, Methodists, Lutherans, Quakers, Shakers, Moravians, Mennonites, Amish, Swedenborgians, Schwenkfeldians, Salzburgers, Unitarians, Adventists. Continual fission, disagreement, separation, political patronage, and alignment seemed to mark the progress of the Reform, to such a degree that Erasmus finally packed up his books and took off for a secret retreat in Switzerland, muttering frostily: "I will put up with the [Catholic] Church, until I find a better one."

America, founded on this new vision of the human Castle, was no less prolific, no less imaginative in its pursuit of autonomy for every conscience, a church for every theory. Americans multiplied, divided, and subdivided. The Baptists alone split into German Baptists, Particular Baptists, Free-Will Baptists, Seventh-Day Baptists, Anti-Mission Baptists, Missionary Baptists, United Baptists, Two-Seed-in-the-Spirit Baptists. The Lutherans were split into the American Lutheran Church, the Lutheran Church in America, and the Lutheran Church-Missouri Synod. Presbyterians formed themselves into the Presbyterian Church in the United States (Southern and Northern) and the Continuing Presbyterian Church. Campbellites split into Disciples of Christ, Church of Christ, and the Christian Church. Adventists, Methodists, and others likewise splintered.

All this came in the wake of a long train of theologians, preachers, self-styled founders, revelators, leaders, and teachers, a list which surely contains some of the most colorful and, at times, the most inventive characters in American history: Richard, Cotton, and Inverse (Face of an Angel) Mather, Roger Williams, Thomas Hooker, George Fox, William Penn, Jonathan Edwards, George Whitefield, Jonathan Mayhew, self-proclaimed female Jesus Mother Ann Lee ("There never was, nor can be, a child conceived and born under Christian auspices"—she fiercely condemned all sexual relations as sinful), Alexander Campbell, circuit preacher Knock-'Em-Down Peter Cartwright, William (the Consecrated Cobbler) Carey, Charles Taze Russel, Joseph Smith, Mary Baker Eddy, Dwight Moody, Billy Sunday (Soaking it into Satan), Charles M. Sheldon (the social gospel), Bruce Barton (the gospel of success), Father Divine ("Peace! it's wonderful!"), Daddy Grace ("Grace has given God a vocation," he said, as he baptized two hundred with a water hose), Bill Bright, Billy Graham, and an entire gaggle of Jesus preachers down to the God-talkers broadcasting over their radio stations throughout the Bible belt of the seventies.

With the central force of the vision so fractionated; with its energies so spent in the constant, unforeseen, and in some cases unbelievable theological and political squabbles and piques, the hoped-for effect of Wittenberg on the meaning and life of the individual had also to be less than men had dreamed when Europe banished the likes of Johann Tetzel. Luther, partisan of the nobility, at heart a medieval man, did aid in prizing states free of papal and clerical control, replacing the old feudal system with primitive capitalist economies. But the violent and bloody support given the Reformers by political leaders such as Christian II of Denmark and Norway, Gustavus Vasa and, later, Gustavus Adolphus of Sweden, Cardinal Richelieu of France, the German Electors, Henry VIII of England, the Swiss Covenanters, and others was only a means for each one's aggrandizement and meant bloody struggles for precious little alteration in the lives of ordinary man. The Reform followed strictly political lines: Germany, England, Switzerland, Scandinavia, and Holland became Protestant with their rulers; and all churches were thoroughly state controlled. Southern European states remained Catholic with their rulers. And neither ever touched the lands of Eastern Orthodoxy.

The ordinary individual in the newly Protestant European states, as in the older Catholic ones, found himself still living in a class society; still restricted in his political possibilities by blood and race; excluded from all upward mobility; his fate in peace as a worker, and in war as cannon fodder still decided by a self-chosen and self-perpetuating elite; perforce sharing the religious bigotry and exclusivism of his rulers; and not freed from superstition and ignorance.

The condition of European common man and woman at the opening of the twentieth century was accurately described in Kafka's *The Castle:* they were human ants and impotent ciphers. Even with the convulsions of the French and Russian revolutions and the year of revolutions, 1848, the people again emerged as ciphers. The great Protestant empires of England, Holland, and Germany rivaled any empire in history for oppression, slavery, robbery, and maintained degradation of native populations. The Wittenberg vision fathered no earthly utopia in Europe or in the hundreds of overseas colonies.

In terms of the individual, the vision transplanted to America had what seemed another beginning, and produced a much happier state of things. One of the quirks of history was that the inheritors of Wittenberg had to flee Europe with its frozen sociopolitical categories in order to attempt their Castle in its full human expression. America, in comparison with Europe, was obviously no less prolific, no less imaginative, in its pursuit of autonomy for every conscience, a church for every theory, an airing for any idea—although some time did elapse before basic freedoms were recognized for the non-Protestant, non-white resident or immigrant. But infusing the early colonies of the seventeenth century and the Continental Union of the eighteenth century, we find the same suspended beauty of the vision as animated the original sixteenth-century visionaries: an expectant feeling that some new condition of human felicity was in the offing, and that it not only should, but would, be characterized by social freedom, a sturdy independence, total liberty to exercise personal reason within wide horizons of life and movement and beneath the umbrella of a divine blessing. After all, people were starting off in a completely new and gigantic land with no constraining hand on them, with everything to build as they wished from zero point. There was a sylvan promise, a vernal note to the early settlements in America, as if the new arrivals were dimly conscious of a great drama about to unfold. It was a fresh land of Canaan, given them by God as to his newly chosen people, in which to build the Castle of Wittenberg.

But, in keeping with the constant contrast of Wittenberg to other visions, it was the first time and the first place that Christianity was imported and imposed on a land without its taking any sustenance from the land's religious tradition. This is a capital trait of the Wittenberg vision in the United States; it may go a long way to explaining the enigma which Protestantism faces today.

A contrasting comparison in such wholesale importing brings out the peculiar nature of religion in the United States. In the same hemisphere, in Mexico, Central and South America, the incoming Christians were *possessed* by the land. Their Christianity fell into the land's ancient articulation. The native gods, goddesses, and spirits were not banished. They were assumed. The Aztec Mictlantecuhutli, the Mayan Hapikern, the Incan Supai, all breathed fire into Christianity's· satan. Beneath the beard of God the Father there shelters Quetzalcoatl, Pohochacyum, and Apu-Punchau. The Madonna assumed the roles of Xilone, of Akna, of Mama Quilla. At Easter time today, the head of a dead cockerel is attached to the Cross of Jesus as he mirrors Huitzilopochil's features beneath his Crown of Thorns. Not only in the high places of Machu Picchu, but around Lake Atitlan and in the village chapels, Pom incense and rubber balls are burned for sun and rain. Christ's mysteries are penetrated with peyote. The Earth Goddess wears Spanish shoes. Lacendon Indians burn copal in honor of the Immaculate Conception. Rain god Chac is a Christian saint. The *Mu Igala* Book is read with *Revelations*. Mayan fertility gods smile for the Chamula Indians, as Saints Felicia, Perpetua, Scholastica, and Dorothea do for the Greeks, Italians, and Spaniards. The painted skulls of the terrible Tlaloc adorn the supper table each Halloween night. And, whether it is Europe or Africa or Asia or Polynesia, the story is the same as in the southern American continent: there has been no break in the land's continuity through its inhabitants from at least 10,000 years ago up to this day.

Not so, up north. No American town or city ever belonged to a god, as Tula to Tezcatlipoca, as Ephesus to Diana, as Athens to Athena, as Rome to Jupiter, as Karachi to Kali, as Jerusalem to Yahweh, as Mecca to Allah, as Corinth to Hercules. When the Indian gods and spirits of America fled, there was no thunder on the plains. Today, you will hear no echoes of Mudjekeewis, Father of the Four Winds, and no voice of the supreme Gitche Manitto, Master of Life, from his Twelfth Heaven. Mary the Virgin shared nothing with Nokomis, Daughter of the Moon. Jesus assumed no roles from Aldebaran. Satan ignored Pauguk, the Death Spirit. Americans smoked the calumet; but Pukwana, its spirit, never became Holy Spirit. The giant Wendigoes never vied with the Saints.

All that is gone. Like the hoof prints of the bison. Like the defunct kingdom of Wabasso. Like the Empire of the Six Nations. In their place, we find only the signs of the Wittenberg vision in America: the Thanksgiving on Plymouth Rock; the riding preacher with Bible in his saddlebags and Hell on his lips; the spare New England steeple; the family Bible; the thumping chant of revivalist meetings; the immigrant church in the big city slum; Thoreau by the quiet of Walden Pond; Billy Graham "confessing" hundreds of thousands for Jesus in Madison Square Garden; Rex Humbard's $2.1 million domed black marble and glass Cathedral of Tomorrow set down among Burger

King, Kentucky Fried Chicken, and Arby's Roast Beef restaurants near Cuyahoga Falls, Ohio; the neo-Gothic cathedrals, and the Sunday drive-ins; the affluent and democratic peace of every Forest Lawn. Only these you find strung along the lines of the American effort.

This independence of the new Americans from the aged articulation of the land they came to occupy seems to have been at the root of the force and momentum which catapulted history out of old molds. For there was a marriage between a visionary ethic and an open-ended political system. Protestantism championed rationalism and rationalization. It developed a characteristic work ethic, the Protestant Ethic, free of mystery, free of myth, free of magic. No one can doubt that it was this basic vindication of human freedom which made American democracy possible; or that it was this unrestrained use of reason, logic, and probing analysis which made twentieth-century science and technology possible. Without the freeing of minds from Roman authoritarianism, without the freedom to be wrong, as well as to be right, Europe—and America—might have gone the way of classical China: attaining a certain humanistic level of culture and a definite knowledge of some of nature's secrets; but never of itself plunging on without restraint to probe, experiment, try again, finally to succeed; never being allowed to push the bounds of factual knowledge beyond the diktat of an ignorant and self-serving authority. The American Union of the eighteenth century bore the traces of the Calvinism which Wittenberg had produced. But this basic Calvinism was leavened by the innate tendency of Protestantism to divide, subdivide, mutate, and change according to the personal conscience and the individual reason of its members.

At the same time, and in practical terms of thought, moral principle, and way of life, it was inevitable that self-regulating and dissenting reason would be turned on the very sources of Wittenberg—the Bible and Christianity. Once individual conscience was granted absolute immunity and reason was declared independent of all control or authority, there was no reason in the world why one could not deny the existence of any god, describe the Bible as a collection of popular stories and legends, regard the Christian Church as nothing more or better than any human organization, and conclude that man was a highly organized biologism devoid of soul or spirit. Human ethics, in that case, would be reduced to the status of practical politics with no religious, much less supernatural, significance. This, in fact, is what happened.

Already in 1642, Lord Herbert had proposed in his *De Veritate* that there had always existed "a natural religion shared by all wise men and women from time immemorial." In the same century, Locke taught that we can use unaided reason to arrive at a natural religion. In the eighteenth century: a Boston preacher, Jonathan Mayhew, proposed to examine the Bible with reason alone; Hume set out to establish that all concepts of a god and of man are derived uniquely from our human sensation; Descartes held that reliable human knowledge comes only in "clear and distinct ideas"—by reason and logic only, therefore; the French Encyclopedists maintained that all human knowledge is ultimately self-explanatory; and Immanuel Kant redefined religion as a closed ethical system over which presided human reason.

These new strains of European intellectualism with their emphasis on reason, on personal experience, and on man's isolation in his universe, were joined to Newtonian physics and harnessed to the continuing discoveries of science as it catalogued the vitals of the physical world. Archeology, linguistics, and anthropology—not only unrestrained by any authoritarian guide but in pointed revolt against any restraint—probed the Bible and Christianity's beginnings. With Voltaire and Rousseau as its voluble and crackling spokesmen, there was on its way a comfortable and defensible mental attitude for all reasonable mortals.

There emerged, therefore, in Protestant Europe and in America from the eighteenth century onward, a transmuted form of the Wittenberg vision which has been called Deism. Many Americans who were vital to the country's formation and to the definition of its future course were Deists: Benjamin Franklin, Thomas Jefferson, Alexander Hamilton, John Quincy Adams, James Madison. Deism, the seasoning if not the broth of the American melting pot, had and still has one basic, unproven, and unprovable assumption: any divine revelation—if it is genuinely divine—must demonstrate to human reason in clear and distinct ideas that it *is*, indeed, divine. With the strong emergence of Deism, and in the name of total freedom of reason and the complete personalization of conscience, the objects of knowledge came to be as strictly defined as they had been in earlier times, but with another emphasis. Now they consisted only of notions which would submit to a rational explanation in clear and distinct ideas, and only facts, that could be demonstrated scientifically by the objective means of quantitative measure. All else must, by objective definition, be irrational, a-rational, superstitious, unnecessary, and ultimately unworthy of a human being.

This, of course, meant that human reason was the measure of all things. Nature was the only real living gospel for men. The aim of human life was that one should be "good." "But," added the Deist humorously, if grimly, "be not righteous overmuch!"

Other transforming agents awaited the Wittenberg vision. Two giants of the nineteenth century forced its inheritors farther on down the road to where they would one day face a life-or-death choice. Charles Darwin had convinced European and American intellectuals, by 1860, that evolution was a fact of history. Fifty years later, Sigmund Freud produced a powerful criticism of all religious belief and all ethical systems based on such beliefs. Traditional ideas of virtue, sin, soul, spirit, god, heaven were reduced to terms not allowed to exceed the fossil remains etched on evolutionary charts or to break beyond the bounds of the new constructs in psychology and psychiatry.

Thus by the middle of the twentieth century, Protestants had moved by a series of steps to the brink of voluntary self-destruction. The first step was to set up personal conscience as the only acceptable norm for conduct and for belief in God. This led them to fractionate and divide into multiple sects with differing beliefs about God and Jesus. The second step was to assert that their reason must approve before they believed in anything proposed to them. This meant that they made their reason the measure of any knowledge about God. The third step was, logically, to reason about God only with the resources of reason. And, because they found much about God inexplicable by reason alone, they concluded that these matters had no significance. Imperceptibly, they concluded that what they could not explain with reason had no reality. So having started off with a vision of themselves as one with nature and God, they ended up alone with nature. God, Jesus, the supernatural, all had stepped out of the picture. And, with them, the vision.

The official bearers of the Wittenberg vision—Protestant churches and leaders—have from time to time attempted to remedy this situation. In earlier times, there were two great "awakenings." The first took fire with the 1734 *Sinners In The Hands Of An Angry God* sermon of

Jonathan Edwards. Initial Revivalist hysteria gave way to solid results: schools and colleges; asylums and societies for the deaf, the mute, the insane, the blind, the helpless, the orphaned; temperance, peace, prison reform became burning issues. By the time of the American Revolution, it was all over. The second awakening (1801) started in Kentucky with two Methodist preachers, spread to Pennsylvania, Virginia, and to much of the nation. By 1830, it was a spent force.

Later in the 1830s, an effort was made to develop a religious fervor compatible with Deism. Some Unitarians detached themselves from their parent group. They called themselves the Transcendental Club. Falsely described as a back-to-nature movement, Transcendentalists professed a mixture of Platonism and Neoplatonism, with elements drawn from European and Oriental pantheism. Ralph Waldo Emerson, their best known advocate, held that "man has access to the entire mind of God," and that "Reason is the highest faculty of the soul, what we often mean by the soul itself." Man is part of "Mind," he said, of "Over-Soul." His saying that "Evil will bless. Ice will burn," displays the Buddhistic trait in his beliefs. But transcendentalism was a vain attempt to leap over the barbed-wire fence of eighteenth- and nineteenth-century rationalism in order to reach a transcendent view. Its "spiritualizing" effort survives today in thinkers and writers such as Buckminster Fuller, William E. Thompson, Abraham Maslow, and Harlow Shapley.

Nearer our day, there have been new and renewed attempts to enkindle faith: a Key '73 Campaign to "reconvert" America; a new book (*Are You Running With Me, Jesus?*); a newly popular preacher; a new slant on religion—the "God is Dead" fad; the popularization of interest in the Dead Sea Scrolls; campus crusades; Pentecostalism; Jesusites; Children of God; ecumenical gatherings; clerical vindication of grape pickers in California, of housing in Milwaukee, of blacks' rights in the South; freshly devised church happenings; wholly new and sometimes bizarre church ceremonies. All to no avail. Even the labors and sometime genius of Paul Tillich, Reinhold Niebuhr, and Karl Barth did nought: they analyzed the problem but provided no solution. Anyway they were not heard. *Jonathan Livingston Seagull* by Richard Bach and *Once Is Not Enough* by Jacqueline Susann were read and meditated by more people than any one of the above giants in theology.

Greater reliance is put, by vastly greater numbers of people, in fluctuating fads such as transactional analysis or primal scream therapy than in any theology. Protestantism for the mass of its adherents, in Europe and in the United States, has become an open-ended Deism which allows for twin possibilities: either that there is *more* than a benign deity or supreme being or supernatural force, more than an impersonal and unattainable ideal "out there"; or this very deity or supreme force is itself a myth—useful, convenient, inspiring even, but wholly imaginary. For their rank and file members, Protestant churches allow this open-ended Deism and recommend certain actions, prayers, concepts specific to each group.

Thus, in the last half of the twentieth century, the inheritors of the Wittenberg vision find themselves standing proud and approaching a point where they may choose, again in contrast to other visions, to pay an unheard-of price in defense of total autonomy of reason and consistent reliance on personal conscience as the criterion of what is humanly good or evil. According to that human reasoning which they so successfully vindicated, the ancient mysticism which gave rise to the Wittenberg vision is impossible. Indeed, according to reason, that knowledge is not factual and, therefore, is mythical; that faith is irrational; and the irrational is not worthy of a thinking man. Even if Jesus came walking on the waters, reason would have its imperial say.

In morality, the Wittenberg vision is even more constrained. For, to obtain a general rule, one must poll the individual consciences; one must rely on a head count. What is good depends on the majority of ayes, what is bad, on a majority of noes. But thus morality becomes a matter of political decision and civil law. In the very effort to find the machinery for allowing groups of mortals to observe that morality, there is a declared end to personal conscience.

Meanwhile, innerliness becomes impossible except in factual concepts and measurable psychological acts. Yet, without innerliness, there is no vision of the human Castle.

Thus the descendants of Wittenberg are perhaps yet again set off in contrast to others; they are perhaps the first to be so fully confronted in life and death terms with the question just beginning to nag at others: why can they no longer detect a divine glow over the steel, concrete, chrome, and cement of our man-made world? The skies have become leaden and impenetrable coverings locking out the desired burst of light. Most Wittenberg inheritors have come to a brink where they might be the first to ask questions in which the life of all mankind's vision resides. With human reason as the only norm, allowing no further recourse, can there ever be a love greater than reason can conceive? With personal conscience as the final rule, can there ever be a law of love greater than the individual conscience allows? Was the hope and trust of Wittenberg born only to be buried with the fossils of animals and the bones of kings? Was the force of the vision and the faith of Wittenberg to have the effect, not of enthroning, but of isolating reason from all the tools of man, and to make of it a burnished tragic burial spade?

But this cannot be the last word about the Wittenberg vision. For the legend of love still twinkles along the edges of the long shadows cast by the inanity of human reason as the only judge of the divine, and around the quicksands of inadequacy engulfing any personal conscience left entirely to its own devices. Protestantism's official advocates—churchmen, theologians, thinkers—are in trailing decline, have almost had their day. But within the Protestant there persists that same undying will which marks his vision. It defies the fate of hopeless entombment, refuses the reminders of human absurdity which he has hitherto collected as bag and baggage. Somewhere between the belly of his desire, the heart of his mortality, and the mind of his metallic logic, he has another organ for loving the eternal unabatedly and for accepting the divine word which inspired his beginnings in the sixteenth century.

And this is the assertive trust you read in stone on the Luther Memorial in Worms. He, the great cog, stands there flanked by some of the other cogs—Reuchlin, Frederick the Wise, Waldus, Melanchthon, Hus, Savonarola, Philip the Great. Artist Ernst Rieschl has personified even the cities of Luther's greatest triumphs. Speyer, Magdeburg and Augsburg. They all assert silently: "Only fierce revolt could have freed us. Therefore we revolted fiercely." But the assertion has an implicit trust. That beyond the brink of suicide proposed to Protestantism, its inert body will suffuse with life. That it will be stirred by divine grace streaming through the labyrinth of its wistful dreams, soothing the hurts and scars, cooling the passion of all Protestant fears. That there will be a resurrection and a nearby talismanic moment free from the gothic darkness of conscience and the long night of imperial reason.

And Protestants can feel again the seedtime and the springtime in redemptive love. They will stand on the doorstep of inner life, in the land of divine morning they knew existed at the moment they began.

9

PERU, INDIANA
Lines of Spirit

Now here in Peru (rhymes with SEE-RUE), north central
Indiana, on the Wabash river, take a long and thoughtful
walk. Southwest on Main Street. Cross northwest at Clay,
leaving the library and museum at your back, until you
reach Broadway Shopping Plaza. Bear southwest on
North Broadway, turning southeast at the court house. Or
walk down by McKrinstry as far as Rosewood, up to Dav-
enport Avenue, out to Mount Hope where Ben Wallace's
monument stands. Travel every horizontal inch of Peru's
sixty-five miles of streets (95 percent paved). You will find
Peru a frame of all America, a statistician's model.

There is no surprise glory in its angular streets. What
human glory is there in the Blinkenfurter typewriter (pat-
ented July 15, 1891), now part of the Puterbaugh Museum in Peru? Nor any burgeoning poetry. What poetry
do you find in the 1870 stagecoach bought by Tom Mix,
now displayed in Miami County Historical Museum?

Almost at the geographical center of the United States,
notes the statistician, the site of Peru (Circus Capital of the

World) emerged from a treaty signed on October 28, 1826 with the Miami (Cry-of-the-Crane) Indians. Platted for William Hood in spring, 1834. Incorporated on February 3, 1847. Height above sea level: 650 feet. Population today: 14,139 (2.4 percent non-white; 99 percent American born). Annual budget: $431,431. Products: cattle, hogs, grain, tomatoes, plastics, basketry, mechanical parts, electronics. Houses: 5207. Companies: 47. Clubs and organizations: 74. One each: airport, hospital, synagogue. Two of many: railroads, dailies, hotels, banks, radio stations, rivers. Three museums and three theaters. Thirty-eight churches.

Chicago is 140 miles northwest, Detroit 224 miles northeast, and Grissom Air Force Base 5 miles due south. As the crow flies, you are 350 miles from southern Appalachia where there is a nightmare as children die from malnutrition; and you are 1400 miles from Las Vegas where there is a dream as a player drops $70,000 at roulette in one evening. You are 620 miles from Wall Street, New York, where men are realists in numbers and paper; and 1920 miles from Big Sur, California, where Zen devotees flee such reality. Peru, Indiana is on the edge of the East, within hailing distance of the Big Diamond and the Midwest, and has a tang of the South.

See this town, not merely as Peru, Indiana. But as Peru, Indiana Plus. Pursue that Plus horizontally and vertically, and you enter the spectrum of American effort strung out in ever-multiplying lines: curving, straight, coiled, looped, snarled, crisscrossed. And in geometric forms: squares, cubes, rectangles, triangles, pentagons, octagons, tetragons. And in numbers: commuters at 8:30 A.M., turnpikes, auto traffic, computer readouts, vital statistics of the nation (172,000 killed by heart attacks, 207,000 killed by strokes in 1969), ticker tape, neat unending furrows of suburban settlements, assembly lines, supermarket displays, credit cards, and the decorative script on the Lockheed Company tie: Lockheedteneleventristarwithrollsroyceengines. And in sound: 24-hour radio, 24-hour airport arrivals and departures, 24-hour roar of the big city.

The landscape of effort in Peru, Indiana Plus is linear, forever linear, is always increasing the lines. Further and further, taller and taller: more numbers, more miles, more people, more objects, more experiments. The lines never stop. In any part of America, it is the same. Expand the lines of Peru, Indiana to the dimensions of the New York-Boston-Washington megalopolis. Contract them to the size of New Hampton, Missouri (population: 432). In all cases, Peru, Indiana mirrors each of them. No building in Peru is higher than the four-story Bell Music Building. In three to five years, all its buildings can be as high as any on Manhattan Island.

Pursue that Plus factor in Peru, Indiana transcendently, and you see all the lines as an index pointing to the American Castle. In that Plus, therefore, see Peru as surrogate of all American settlements whose "sharp names," as Stephen Benet said, "never get fat": New York, New York; Lickskillet, Tennessee; Blue Ball, Pennsylvania; and Atlanta, Georgia; Cut And Shoot, Texas; Los Angeles, California; Palm Beach, Florida; and Bowlegs, Arizona. Everywhere, in fact, that the American being is celebrated in horizontal and vertical effort, you will see at a glance the long, leaping parabola of the America covenant locked as to its lodestar onto a totally new Castle vision. The New World. They named it well.

In comparing it with other Castle visions, it is easier to say what the American vision is not rather than what it is, what it does not include than what it does include. Land roots, for instance. In Peru, Indiana, no ancient gods whine in cellars beneath the foundations of Canterbury

House at Clay and Canal. The street names (Fremont, Walnut, Benton, Shields, Buckeye . . .) are not resonances of deep-seated tribal instincts; and even the few Indian place names which survive ring with no cultic memories or eternal moments lived long ago—Maconaquah (Little Bear Woman), Tah-king-gah-me-con-gi (Running Water Place). No wan goddess buried under City Hall between East Third and Second weeps for ruined shrines where once her oracles were changed; native son Cole Porter (his apartment at Huntington and East Third is now a duplex) sang, but of things American. Native son Emil Schram was president of the New York Stock Exchange. Peru's great men are definitely not mythical.

No blocks from bygone altars line East River Street. No annual feast day masks an ancient rite; the July Circus (the Hagenbeck-Wallace Circus winters here) is pure Barnum & Bailey. No river gods hide beneath the names Wabash (White Flat Rock) and Mississinewa (Water on the Slope). The city is centered around no dusty monument. (Anthony Wayne's shaving kit and Mark Twain's goggles are displayed in the Puterbaugh Museum.) There is no venerated tomb (Francis Godfrey, last War Chief of the Miamis, is buried one-half mile south of the intersection between State 124 and the Frances Slocum Trail). There is no place where mysteries were once celebrated by Little Turtle and Tecumseh (this was their area) in honor of a kingly sun or an exigent moon.

There is nothing meandering or jigsaw or piggyback about it all, nothing of aristocrats' whimsy or poetic license to be read in its contours. It is a rather geometric north-south, east-west arrangement. For convenience. For mobility. For tearing down. For replacing. For expanding. For deserting.

And so it is also in Peru, Indiana Plus. There never were national gods and goddesses, never an American pantheon of spirits. Never a public, official priestly caste of the nation. Whatever God or gods and goddesses are to be found in America are imports and out of all articulation with the land and its past. Even the devils of North Berwick and New Salem were merely cut-rate campers from Europe, Africa, and the Orient. Americans permitted themselves only one peculiarly American feast day: Thanksgiving (immediate connotation: turkey with stuffing, cranberry sauce, and pumpkin pie). Their ghosts are heroes dead in real battles or historical leaders remembered for their acts. Americans never had a mythology formed by ancients, handed down, honed, and refined by their cultural and religious history, appearing and reappearing until celebrated in their very language and customs and in their national mentality. The cowboy was never mythic; embroidered, he made great material for films and category novels. The nearest thing to American folk music comes in the hillbilly songs and the black strain. They, and whatever folkloric handcrafts there are, were imported.

For this land did not prolong its own primeval being in the new arrivals. Rather, the land was assumed by them in their helter-skelter pursuit of a dream. No one of them became an articulation of the land's ancient liturgy. The land became theirs. They never became the land's, as Frenchmen are Lorraine's, as Sicilians are Sicily's, as Englishmen are England's, as Afghanis are Afghanistan's. Their thinking and their hoping, their talking and their believing, their traveling and their building were never colored by the land's ageless hues of fear, hope, life, and death. All these were dazzled over by the newcomers, colored by fourscore "isms," filtered through almost as many nationalisms as Europe and Asia contained. And, yet, the vision elaborated here is colored in its essence by none of these.

It was to be a land of "fustests" and "greatests" and "mostests"—noble, banal, ordinary. Peru, Indiana used to have (1905) the largest and most costly ($20,000) hand-mixed cement bridge (on East Riverside Drive) in the world. Peru, Indiana Plus has the costliest ($1 million) public toilet in the world (Texas); and there were forty million cars (the whole population of France) on the road during Labor Day weekend of 1973. But these, just as the tallest building, the first moon landing, or any other firsts, are no more than side effects of the purpose of coming to America.

Those who came to become Americans, who molded and still mold Peru, Indiana Plus, came because of a Castle vision. They had seen it in England, Germany, Ireland, Poland, Russia, Spain, Hungary, Tunis, Italy, Lebanon, Armenia, Turkey, and elsewhere. They would seek that vision on, not find it in, this land. The land for them was "unstoried, artless, unenhanced." That is why the men who work at the C & O Railroad north of U.S. 24 and at the Sewage Plant on West 24th, the women shopping on Broadway, the children singing at the Peru Community Junior High, and the twenty-six cops in the five patrol cars who keep the peace have nothing deeply in common with Europeans, Africans, Asians, and Latin Americans—as far as vision goes. London Bridge is now in Lake Havasu, Arizona. San Simeon Castle is now in California. But not as memories. Nor as mementos. Rather, as showpieces of a past they do not seek to reproduce. Not trophies of bygones; rather, milestones left behind long ago by people who are in hot pursuit of a vision not mirrored in any one of their pasts but which has yet to be achieved.

At the same time, the very possession of the dream as part of each American's life seemed to guarantee to them that they were not of this universe as either the sticks and stones and seas and stars, or as the animals and plants and physical forces, or as beings tradition bound, class bound, or race bound. But simply as humankind. The relation of Americans not only to the land but to one another and to their past and future was new on the human horizon.

Their effort was to create a new environment. On the land as they found it molded by the Indians, the stars were the campfires of the tribes in the sky, the earth was the turtle floating on an endless sea, and every place was sacred to a spirit as was every living thing. But they, the newcomers, would travel to the stars and beneath the sea as well as on it; they would make the earth over to their bent; and they would regard every other thing as matter for their efforts. So they buried the land's past together with the shell cups, wampum beads, gorgets, stone pipes, tomahawks, peace treaties. And the last bearers of the land's articulation they hustled off to reservations. The rule: no assimilation with the past of this land or of any other. In New York City, that effort buried Kapsee (Sharp Rock Place) beneath Battery Park and the towers of Wall Street, the tepee villages of the Canarsee beneath the apartment houses of the Silk Stocking District, and the foodpits of the Weekquaesgeek beneath the Garment District. Minna-atn (Island of Hills) became Manhattan, forest of soaring skyscrapers. It was always the effort.

In America, to merely external examination, the effort appeared to be simply economic: dollars, industries, the good life. The 1810 economic census of the United States said: "There are 1 million families and 1 million slaves. An average homestead is worth $300, an average slave $400." Total value of the United States then: $3 billion. In 1973, the gross national product was $1 trillion and the total worth of the United States (at 5 percent earnings) about $20 trillion. Of all blacks, 50 percent had entered middle class status. There were 15 million (imagine the whole population of Holland) on welfare. "What's good for General Motors is good for the country," Charlie Wilson had said. "And there's 'a little bit of Union Carbide in every home,' " added the man in shirtsleeves quoting a former ad slogan of that company. But all this should be seen as part of the effort.

In that effort for the new Castle vision, America in its polity and way of life resembled nothing more closely than a gigantic sieve: receiving a rain of varieties, multiplicities, idiosyncrasies, localisms, ideologies, traditions, outlooks; ceaselessly winnowing and straining them all as they balanced for a day, a year, an epoch; continually sifting and shaking, letting them all in their turn tumble through the taut and thin meshes of the linear ideal. For those sharp lines have held and will hold nothing but the reflection of the beckoning vision. Sometimes, what was thrown into the sieve seemed bound to hold there, to stop its dynamic shifting, to weight it down to the ground. Yet, the sieve always has proved more powerful. "No matter what you throw at us," quips actor Sidney Poitier to an American Nazi in a World War II movie, "this country is big enough to nail it firmly to the ground."

One of the most persistent factors thrown into the great sieve was Christianity's ethic or moral code as developed in Europe between 500 and 1500 A.D.: what it meant in human terms to be a morally good or morally bad man or woman. The basic tenet of that code: all human morality depends on a formal religion—its beliefs, institutions, ministers, rules, liturgy, authority, bible, traditions. The basic implication of that code: some human beings (implicitly, Christians) were enlightened, were the chosen—in America's case, were exclusively white, predominantly Protestant.

As a consequence, there arose concrete attitudes. According to some of these, rights were initially denied to non-whites, non-Protestants, women, youth, children. Parental authority, male preeminence, capital punishment were championed. Other attitudes affected the sexuality of the individual: homosexuality, contraception, abortion, polygamy, promiscuity, open-ended marriages were forbidden. Others proscribed mercy killing, suicide, experiments on human beings—the fetus or fully developed persons. Others still created canons of pornography, obscenity, lewdness, patriotism, decency.

Again, there was a whole body of attitudes within this moral code that concerned overall views of man: as created by a god; endowed with an inner conscience—thus creating his guilt or innocence; bound to work for his living and thus "perfect" himself, either sinning or doing "good" during his life; and, on dying, consigned to punishment in "Hell" or reward in "Heaven." Yet, no specific trait of that traditional Christianity could stand up to the continual sieving and straining; and no particular brand of Christianity ever took predominant hold over this new people. Apparently, none of them as expressions of religious instinct was suitable for the American vision of the Castle.

It has taken almost two centuries; but now, approaching their two-hundredth anniversary, Americans have almost discarded that Christian ethic as typically American. Most religious elements are gone from public life. Some of the moral and moralizing attitudes have changed completely. Others, such as mercy killing (53 percent in a recent Gallup poll favor one or other form of it), monogamy (open-ended marriages are in), fetus experimentation (recently proposed by an officer of the powerful and conservative American Medical Association), patriotism (in its older form), are under severe examination and revision. And, increasingly, any trace of Christian belief or practice (e.g., school prayer) is banished by law from public life.

Apparently, the American outlook does not brook coloration derived from any particular religious belief, any mythology, any cultural emphasis. In a space of almost two hundred years, a variety of old and new forms of worship and belief—Christian and non-Christian—have flourished in America. Now they all stand side by side, each claiming its limited number of adherents. Every one of them is a part of the visible scene. All of them line the ways along which the people move. But the outlook accepted as American is not identifiable with any of them in particular.

It is as if Americans, behind and above their political union, had an unspoken covenant with a vision of loveliness all their own. Unspoken and unwritten. Not with land or with church; not with philosophy, culture, civilization. Not even with life, much less with death. Seemingly, it is a covenant with their humanness as a group. Not humanness, however, as an abstract concept of nature or a detailed dogma of religion, or a static quantum preserved and treasured like the Crown Jewels. But that quality of humanness born among individuals freely compacting together to create a condition for themselves colored only by the ideal of constant betterment through action, through doing. So that men of differing religions, diverse cultures, different civilizations, even divisive philosophies, could pact together and stay together; all, by that act, participating in that humanness and its blessing. So that whatever may be humanly good in the broadest sense in their particularities and individualisms will flow into and swell that commonwealth of goodness. But anything in them which derives solely from localisms (outlooks tied to one land) and parochialisms (outlooks self-limiting to some men and women) would be excluded. In that vision of humanness lies the uniquely American vision of the Castle.

The loveliness of that vision is not such as the natural

beauty of our world pours in through our senses, eliciting emotional images, imaged thoughts, felt reasons, and the long, long daydreams of our mortal compassion, fear, and hope for togetherness uninterrupted by death or fatigue or boredom. Nor is it any loveliness echoing whatever beauty lingers in the creeds and formularies of a pat religion, in the appanage of a vibrant nationalism, or in the glory of a prosperous empire.

The vision's loveliness is rather of a human being as no man's serf but every man's fellow. Not controllable by any dimensions of human power but nevertheless destructible by sufficient power. Not measurable by hand or eye and their adjunct agencies. It is loveliness that resides in the peculiar humanness that flourishes within a person as the core of his innerliness. Not conceivable by human logic, nor reached as a conclusion of human reasoning. But a loveliness that makes all logic human, all reasoning beautiful, all measurements humanly acceptable, all dimensions of human power bearable. Expressed in this vision in actions. Not in words, which confine. Not in theories, which blind. But, much as we experience and recognize the reality of kindness in acting kindly, love in a kiss, compassion in tears shed for another's pain, greatness in greatly achieving.

According to the American covenant, we experience and recognize our humanness within the dynamic of our ever-more perfectible condition in ever-more perfectible surroundings, according as we humanize those conditions. This vision does not tolerate action for action's sake (though it must stand up to the criticism throughout the world for what that world mistakenly sees as not merely restless but often blind flailing in a shop full of delicate china). Nor is it work for work's sake. Nor is it the Protestant ethic—which, as one commentator wrote, has found its happiest home in Japan (and, it can be added, in West

Germany). But it is action and work as vehicle of the individual's humanness and active participation in the American covenant.

For the prime presumptions of the covenant are clear. That such a humanness would be good, supremely good, never evil. That it was open ended to the divine and the infinite. And that America had nothing less than a special endowment, a blessing specific to the American union as distinct from all copies, imitations, and extensions. Not the infallibility claimed by the pope. Not the impeccability ascribed to the Virgin Mary by Roman Catholics. Not the immutability described as God's. But a destiny: to establish the lines of human environment where no manmade myth or tradition or image would color the speech and the love of the divine in its approaches to men. On a rich and beautiful earth, men should strive by actions (not philosophy, nor even culture) to humanize it all, thereby striving for the divine and the infinite; never arriving—for the prize is not in such a finite goal; always striving.

Hence the ribaldry which need not be banned as a threat but can enter for a time as part of American dreaming: Mickey Mouse shaking hands with Leopold Stokowski in *Fantasia*, *Playboy* published in Braille, record making in banana eating, and Pat Paulson running for President in 1968. Hence the perpetual tension between the passing now and the inevitable next, between the fleeting todays and the pursuing tomorrows. Better tomorrows. And tomorrow is today. And all is possible, always: a new solution, a finer method, a more elegant answer, a bigger building, a more efficient instrument. The line of perfectibility is infinite.

From the beginning there was a perpetual striving for a moral practice and an outlook that would shake free of any particular coloration; a placing of happiness in eternal striving, a perpetual self-betterment. The ideal lay in the effort of pursuing the ideal. The happiness always to be achieved by perpetual achieving, in a febrile and ever-changing, go-getting impetus.

This perpetual striving and constantly changing achievement is, by almost perfect analogy, reproduced in the changing face Americans have thrown over the landscape of their continent. Now, after an unrestrained, almost wild, initial period of experimentation and development reflecting nearly every form devised by the human mind in the past, one style is beginning to dominate. And, again, this style appears as uncolored and as forward looking. With straight lines and circles and angles that seem to grow, as from roots, from the linear streets of Peru, Indiana Plus; with plane and solid figures; with computers and drills; with calculus and rulers; with synthetic colors and composite substances; men are reaching for a form of beauty that will override time, even though what they build is quickly eroded by the sharp teeth of time's transiency.

In the beginning, their buildings were a rich and memory-full medley: the two-story medieval East Anglia house and the steeply roofed Flemish cottage fathering the low, wide-roofed Dutch colonial, the American shingle, and the ground-hugging Cape Cod styles; in the Southwest, Indian adobe combining with Spanish mission to produce the California ranch house; Georgian and Federal styles followed by the "Greek revival," the fabulous Greek revival, when banks looked like marble temples of ancient Greece, the homes of the Cotton Kingdom had sumptuous Corinthian and simple Doric columns and Greek bathrooms, and the largest Greek-style building in the world (Philadelphia Museum of Art) arose; a Romantic period when anything went—Tuscan villas, Swiss Gothic mansions complete with gables, dormers, and finials, neo-medieval chapels, Gothic clubhouses, octagonal Oriental mosquelike residences; and, later, breweries in Victorian baronial; tramcar depots in neo-Tudor; railway stations in French colonial and Romanesque.

As described on paper and as seen throughout the land, it seems to have been an unwilled, undirected, and aimless growth. An effort without the guiding formation of a human dream. An overgrowth from a surfeit of energy and money, dictated by economics and finance only.

The almost irreverent way in which the recently built was torn down, to be replaced by the equally temporary and soon to be torn down is magnificently exemplified in the fate of the giant ferris wheel of 1893: 264 feet high, carrying sixty passengers in thirty-six cars, it made one million dollars at the Chicago Fair of 1894 and over a quarter of a million at the St. Louis Fair of 1904; it was then dynamited into scrap.

Those who built Agia Sofia in Constantinople and the men and women who built Chartres Cathedral in the 1100s all worked with an antecedent vision in their mind's eye. They put their monuments together piece by piece. But the blueprint of what they intended to exhibit in stone and line and color and glass was already complete for their spirit. They wished, literally, to enshrine it. Not bypass it or nudge toward it. To reproduce it for their senses, rather. To establish a living temple for a past revelation, a permanent roof for the divine that had visited them, an abiding locality of achieved mystery. Not a one-night caravanserai or a way station in an on-rushing quest.

Clearly, the designers and builders of All America designed and built with a view to surpassing what they achieved. Each achievement was a step to another step. It was onward. Forever onward. By the 1880s, cities had blossomed into geometrically arranged lines of balloon-frame houses. By the 1960s, the face of America had become strewn with settlements—towns, cities, suburbs—

along intertwining cement and asphalt lanes of banality: angled streets of stores, offices, gas stations, cinemas, laundromats, hotels, motels, bars, supermarkets, warehouses, dwellings, factories, depots; bristling with TV antennae, electric pylons, telegraph poles. All built for utility. All built to be torn down and replaced. "Bungaloid" growth, as one commentator called it. Even our Historic Buildings. In 1934, 12,000 of these were listed; in 1966, half of those had been demolished.

In the middle of this ever-changing monotony, the shape of the future appeared meaningfully. First in the Home Insurance Building of Chicago—the first steel-frame skyscraper, with supporting walls; then in the Tacoma Building, with nonsupporting walls. Now, edging into the seventies, that linear shape—the iron-gridded finial shooting up from American vitality as from a fabulous and hidden heart of effort and hope—is invading and taking over the external man-made shape of America. It appears in the engineered symmetry of the long-span suspension Delaware Memorial Bridge, the steep skylines of Houston, Texas and Manhattan Island; in the finned rocket carrying man's dreams of penetrating the seas of space, as well as in the bullet-nosed jet engine of our airplanes; in household fixtures, fountain pens, lampstands, textile designs, as in wallpapers, men's ties, women's scarves, and children's day-care centers. And, from the United States it has traveled abroad and can be seen in the jungle of high-rise apartment houses, hotels, and business offices standing on the skyline of Benidorm, Spain, of Beirut, Lebanon, of Singapore in Malaysia, of Caracas, Venezuela, and of Paris, France.

It is a style springing from fresh fibers and new techniques; it is born from men's brains and hands for one purpose: to control power. All is free of any ornament or complication of esthetic beauty; it evokes no poetry or inner meaning. New gleaming materials are fashioned into exciting shapes of precision and speed, more resplendently bright, clean, and functional than the feathers in an eagle's wing—but not exciting any sense of his effortless beauty. The tightly packed patterns of a computer memory bank have 140,000 tiny magnetic ferrite cones formed into a more purposefully intricate system than the arteries of a rose petal or the eddying rings of an oak tree. But without the mystic sheen of the one or the venerable silence of the other. The Transfer-matic machine performs six hundred eighty-eight jobs in manufacturing cylinder blocks smoothly, uniformly, untiringly. But they are fashioned to the lilt of no man's singing; and, when born, they carry the imprint of no human hands. The control panel of an automated oil refinery is a triumph of abstraction. But it does not romance the will with desires of heavenly sleep nor tantalize the mind with shapes of the eternal.

At times, novelists, sometimes poets, even philosophers have written of the new style of reactors, jet engines, electronic brains, hydraulic drills, the vacuum tube, as if these were wombs of poetry and beauty. They use the language fashioned by men of another age whose sensibilities were aroused by a circumambient nature lushly overpowering, masterful in its inimitable intricacy, and beyond challenge by men's intellects or strength, commanding all man's inner yearnings. The atom splitter at Oak Ridge, Tennessee is described as a whirling dancer. The atomic fuel elements mounted on a metal grid submerged in blue-green fluid are viewed as a totem pole. But all such efforts are factitious. A nostalgic pretense. Like throwing a fourteenth-century Flemish cloth-of-gold over the gleaming vitals of a fusion reactor and celebrating the result in a Shakespearean sonnet. Many of us still have residual wishes, vestiges of an irrevocable past. But General Motors will not champion the harmony of mankind and nature. General Electric will not propagate a belief in beauty and virtue.

As many wistful anthropologists tell us, in modern America we will look in vain for a birth of imagery—as men and women once knew it and used it and lived by it. The East River Drive in New York is in no sense a "rolling canyon" mystically descended from the Grand Canyon; one is not an ikon of the other, any more than Main Street in Peru, Indiana or Johnson Boulevard of Houston, Texas reproduces the canyon's grandeur. A glance along the shores of Lake Erie from Buffalo to Cleveland and on to Detroit draws from factory chimneys and warehouses no poetry about human habitation and no lyricism from suburban spreads and inner city ghettos about "what beauty the hand of man hath stolen from the heavens and made his home." Nor can downtown Peru any more than downtown Manhattan be called the "forest of our hopes" or an extension of the great sequoias in California, as if those stark skyscraper oblongs, rectangles, and squares with their thousands of little sightless eyes continued the history encircled in the aged trunks of Yosemite National Park and reproduced the moss-festooned maple trees that clothe Olympic Peninsula, Washington.

Lament though many will (and do already), according as we perfect the physical conditions of life with our patient science and precious factual knowledge, we dissipate the shadows and the sheen of natural contours. A flickering candle or even a nineteenth-century gaslight left room for imagination. No one can ecstasize over a 60-watt bulb. The John Hancock Building in Chicago is not a Mesopotamian ziggurat, nor the Seattle Needle an Egyptian stele, nor the twin towers of New York's World Trade Center the pillars of Hercules; nor the winter quarters of the Hagenbeck-Wallace Circus of Peru a Renaissance palazzo.

We are resolving our surroundings into a calculated

network of straight lines we have measured and of circles we have drawn. The whole is becoming a more or less efficient grid along whose jointed limbs of metal and concrete we transport our goods, we travel, we speak, and we see from afar. Eventually, we think and imagine and love and live and die uniquely within that grid. And no one can tell us, adds the coroner of our dead culture, to see it all as a spiritual arabesque through which we can glimpse the face of God, as men once dreamed.

Still, there is no "getting back to nature"; no fleeing our cities, our systems, our urban mosaic, to find a freshly primeval fire in sylvan surroundings; no psychedelic refuge within our own consciousnesses. No flight even back to an older Castle vision whose only comfort is familiarity. Walden II, materially and mentally, is impossible for Americans. For the course of the effort is inexorably onward.

It is onward to greater and greater control, manipulation, and finally a fashioning of the human environment by humankind. It must be so. There can be no reinstallation of ancient situations, no revival of anciently valued leisure modes of living, a nice balance between a vibrantly mechanized life and a country refuge where we can get away from it all. Unlike Edward in Robert Granat's *Regenesis*, who has tried everything (shock treatment, drugs, suicide, priests, psychotherapy, orthodox worship—anything to dispel his agony and to find the hope necessary for his humanness) and finally succeeds at a group therapy session, our agony will continue unabated.

The mechanization will continue unabated. The systematization with systems and according to systems will go on and on and on and on and on. In every visible and perceptible department of human life. Rural factories will be absorbed by faceless conglomerates. Individual thumbprints on life, those of woodcutters, tinkers, millers, coopers, blacksmiths, carpenters, family doctors will be wiped out to be replaced by the stamped trademarks of efficient machines. And, if we remain at the surface, we will suffer: the worst it can offer will seem worse than death; the best it can offer will seem just not enough to live by.

At its worst, and remaining at the surface, it will surround us with the sameness of the linear city. In this condition, we would feel as pawns of a power which emanates from an eminently successful socioeconomic system built on an endlessly perfectible technology, fed by the physical sciences and stimulated by the biggest consumer society in history. Our American scene would then be construed as an Armageddon of humanness, a wide field set down amid the silent mountains of lost hopes and vain yearnings, where the humans were being slowly crowded into narrow corners by advancing steel coils and mechanical controls; and where the looming bulk of faceless buildings mushroomed irresistibly swallowing every trace of nature, of natural man, as an ant hill encases the ants, as the pyramids entombed the living dead. America would be an organized graveyard of humanness.

At its best, and still at the surface, we will be exposed to a new set of constructs. Sit by waterpools lined with creamy travertine. Enter lobbies walled with specially glazed bricks and permanent enamels. Mount white terrazzo staircases suspended on pencil-thin stainless steel rods. Walk at evening time by the light of mercury vapor lamps shedding a mantle of fleckless green translucence. For machines will give birth to more machines under the other-than-human direction of still other machines. The seasons of our coming years will flow through an ever-changing landscape linked brokenly by no seasons of nature but by chains of created colors stippled with a vast fermentation of not beautiful, but not ugly forms: opposites matched, variations welded, contraries compared, divisions united, angles and circles, squares and dots, points and lines; all flowing with each other in astonishing apposition. We will be in tension between our ambition leaping Castleward and the frozen categories of still-surviving ancient traditions strung out on the struts of Peru, Indiana Plus.

The generation before us marveled at the shining sea of a western sunset at the foot of purple mountains, at the suffusion of a white blue dusk lazing over green inland waters. And in these things they celebrated their humanness. But we will marvel at the fluorescent lighting of General Motors' Technical Center at Warren, Michigan. And this for us will be to find out that there are 56 miles of tubing serviced by 375 miles of wire and 12 miles of fluor ducts. Even so recent an inspiration as Frank Lloyd Wright provided is dead; his cultural presence is gone. The shapes and forms of our building will not have journeyed from the depths of time. They will be molded with the boldness of the drawing board, not with the symbolic thrust of folkloric fantasy. They will not express in any way the essence of our place, our land. Our place names will not be carriers of deeply primordial meaning: Chicago (Odor of Strong Onions) is paramount as name in Peru, Indiana Plus. And can such express the essence of humanness on this land as Americans have conceived it?

Between the log cabin on the Western frontier in 1835 and the moonshot gantry on Cape Canaveral in 1972 there is an indelible line of identity: both are the flimsy and transitory houses of the American hope. Both are shapings of the linear city. They express power but do not reflect beauty. They grip the mind but do not exalt the spirit to contemplation. Neither is a mirror image of mortal man's immortality but merely a wayside station of his effort. Both are primarily (and ultimately) functional: to get to some other and further place from which one will go on further, further, further.

And if they and they alone constitute the paradigm of the American Castle vision at its best, then Americans are doomed to be strung out on the chicken wire of a linear framework, ingloriously "crucified" like Jesus Christ Superstar. They will be glued together merely by plastic signs for A & W Root Beer and McDonald's Hamburgers—from coast to coast. Their hopes will have been vain illusions: once strong winds of the spirit blew and passed through it all. Their ideals will appear as the unreliable afterglow of the spirit's burning thrust, a scattering of effects in the wake of the spirit's passage through the wasteland forest of chrome, steel, concrete, plastic, sound, and speed that Peru, Indiana Plus will have become.

What stupefies many—almost hypnotizing them into a blindness for (and therefore pessimism about) the Castle vision is the apparently negative character of it all. They see the individual within a series of negations. Not the target of an "ism." Not the subject of an ideology. Not colored by any mythology. Not tributary to a formulated canon of morals. Not the required devotee of a religious belief. Not the result of a group culture. Not conditioned by any exigent mental formula. Not the prisoner of an exigent dogma. Not frozen in class molds. Free in body, in mind, in speech, in association, in work, in life, in death. All true, as far as they go. But these only delineate a kingdom of freed and willful atoms, a gaggle of individual solipsisms. Anarchy by definition.

One might become mesmerized by a scene filled with lurid events. All big *A's*. A longest war. A galloping inflation. A nasty energy crisis. A rising price index. A wobbling stock market. A Watergate. A climbing crime rate. A weakened presidency. A sexual permissiveness. A pollution problem. A mass of corruption. Records, all of them. And a scene echoing with lugubrious comments and cries. Said Chairman Arthur Burns of the Federal Reserve Board: "Something has happened to our system of responses. Troubled times have left a psychological mark. . . . Americans are disturbed." (My God, we *are* a case of group schizophrenia, comments the psychologist.) "Marilyn was the last of the myths to thrive in the long evening of the American dream," wrote Norman Mailer. (My God, the man says America is in the evening of its life, gasps the commentator.) "Put your hand on the television screen," instructs Oral Roberts, "and be HEALED." (Evangelism is a billion-dollar industry, notes the man in shirt-sleeves. Halleluja! Come and be conned.) And, in order to get high, writes Edward Rosenfeld, Americans now have 252 ways: from visceral awareness, Mudra, Zen power yell, Zen morning laugh; through synactics, ampernistics, bio-energetics, and transactional analysis; right down to the nitty-gritty of nude therapy and prolonged masturbation. The high: see, hear, and think more clearly; feel more deeply; and get more out of life. An anarchy of yearning.

Or one might be equally frozen in the grip of the present vast hush, the inner hesitation brought on by some stark realizations. That no form drawn from the long attic of American memory fits the present, forecasts the future. That the mere rule of law will not mean an efflorescence of the spirit. That neither economic power, nor financial sinews, nor technological prowess in themselves spell either decadence or bloom. That no traditional answers suffice any longer—indeed, that for Americans they never did. That over the high-rise blocks of Peru, Indiana Plus, through its angular streets and avenues, within the unbeautiful power of the turrets and towers in its business areas, around the steadily unsurprising facades of its comprehensive shopping centers, and throughout the planned infertility and willed sameness of its suburban forests, there will be no light shining as seers saw it, and no voice sounding as we hear it from our ancient books and formularies.

But what looks like American anomie and what sounds like the brouhaha of desperate spirits cloaks the profound issue being decided: whether Americans will trust their vision. For, from the start, what has been apparently guiding Americans in their quest for the Castle has never been defined by their philosophies; none of their religious institutions has ever appropriated it; and none of their political cycles has ever prostituted it: that special lodestar is a unique dimension whose ingredients are spirit and love. But spirit and love not as preached in pulpits or read in catechisms; rather in some way felt as inner to individual Americans to varying degrees and inner to Americans as a societal grouping. There is a deep persuasion that love has made all things possible, that a great love fathered America, still feeds its energies, and justifies its onward effort. And there is an odd and unspoken knowledge of spirit. Not *the* spirit. Not the *Holy Spirit*. Not *a* spirit. Just as we speak not of the matter, or of the physical matter, nor a matter, but simply of matter as a prime ingredient of our tangible universe, so Americans have always assumed spirit as a prime ingredient of their human universe.

That inner dimension of love and spirit is unique. And it is independent both of the charisma of individual leaders and of whatever sociopolitical structures and institutions have evolved over a space of nearly two hundred years. These structures were created to house for a time the inner American dimension,—to afford it expression and a relatively orderly flow. Individual leaders and peer groups come and go according to the exigencies of particular moments, but they do not appropriate this flowing vision.

For this people seems to be the living proof of a truth

yet to be learned by the wide world and to which Americans are only now awakening: that, as a Castle vision reflects in part something greater than the merely human and transitory, so it can never be a static condition. Captured and expressed in their life as a polity is the idea that the human Castle is not a given quantum achieved once and for all at fixed coordinates of time and space.

By now, Americans are locked into a course of action calculated to produce what in history has never been witnessed: a social and political organization of some millions of men, women, and children, whose commonality is unparticularized, but whose individuality flourishes in a thousand singular garbs: in whom individual freedom waxes through colorful, even exotic, always stubbornly self-chosen ways, but whose mutuality in spirit is enriched and diversified—never riven or split—by each component and singular part. It is a dream of humanness outstripping Plato's Republic in warmth and More's Utopia in pragmatism. And it is an untried experiment in greatness. No other greatness seems possible to the American vision of the Castle.

IO

THE NEW CASTLE

The vision of the new Castle has already appeared to millions of men and women throughout our modern world. Not in images and not with concepts, but without intermediaries and directly to their inner selves; for there is no other way open to such a vision. Like previous Castle visions, it promises a substance for their hopes, an answer to their doubts, and a new way of knowing and living. Its greatest harbinger is the dislocation we daily witness more and more in our political affiliations, social structures, establishment outlooks, personal morality, and life values.

For the moment, this dislocation is all most of us can know of the new vision, given our modern approach to reality. We have been taught not to recognize any vision. Only the self in us can do so; but we have learned also to deny that self's existence or to dissect it into "parts," and in any case to tune out from the knowledge it alone can afford us. We *unknow* it, and therefore we cannot respond to what it perceives. Nevertheless, the new vision goes on looming ever larger in the unknowing perception of more and more people; and in the increasing discomfort of its early thrall many would deny the vision's existence or explain away its effects.

Together with this difficulty, we have one other: before the vision becomes a visible and tangible reality, we cannot put its outlines into words; we cannot conceptualize its qualities. For our words and concepts now are hewn only in terms of what is visible and tangible.

We can, though, begin to describe the vision in its happening; and, having revisited the scenes of former visions in order to catch their essences as partial analogies, we can endeavor now to trace the workings of the new vision in our modern world, perhaps even to comprehend its meaning; though it is exactly our understanding of meaning which has gone awry, while our wills remain transfixed with desires that would lift the dust and shambles off the world scene and leave the object of all our wishes bare to human vision.

Our sense of dislocation must, paradoxically, be the same as that of many past onlookers of the human scene, as they witnessed the unfolding of one or other Castle vision in Mecca, Jerusalem, Rome, Constantinople, Angkor Wat, and Pekin. They had been used to a relatively changeless face in the world around them. In Europe, Africa, Australasia, and the Americas, they normally saw large groups of human beings on the treadmill of an established way of life. The landscape fashioned over a long past dictated the framework within which they all lived and sought to maintain, while the cycles of seasons, years, and centuries rolled on and spent themselves over the unchanging shores of human affairs. But, at certain places and at particular times, as we have seen, the whole dimension of human living seemed to overturn. There was each time some very peculiar human implosion followed by a total revamping of man's living dimension, creating eddies of cultural exaltation, social adaptation, political renewal, all of them felt for hundreds, usually thousands, of years afterward and far beyond the epicenter of the original happening. That human implosion, affecting both simple individuals and sizable groups, is what we have called a vision of the human Castle.

Such a vision, when it has come, has always dissolved instantaneously without noise or foreknowledge an entire inner landscape formed in men and women over previous millennia of living. In its place, there has appeared an unexpected landscape, new and impatient of any fallow time. A hidden transom opened in human skies; the infinite, the divine smiled down with utter ease; and a connection was made between the merely natural and the fully human— the grace of the impossibly beautiful.

The human dimension itself was changed. The individual as well as the group at the greatest moment of any vision seems to have shared awe and wonderment in unexpected surroundings which shone with a fresh light making all things new, and sounded with harmonies of living never heard. It bubbled over with a hope-filled zest that made all tomorrows possible; each day became forever, and every yesterday remained as treasure to gild the household of humanness.

So new was the landscape of each new Castle vision that its only portent was a deep and nearly universal yearning, a sense of dislocation between that which was and that which was about to be. In each case, some imageless force gripped men and women, thrusting them beyond all reason and memory and image, far outside any plan predictable from or inculcated by their past. The results—always concrete, never abstract—were surprising, unforeseeable, empirically unmistakable. The inexorable takeover of the Roman Empire by an obscure Christianity is seen by modern sociologists and historians as fixed on the coordinates of historical decay and social evolution. But there was no sudden decay and collapse of the Roman Empire, except in the imagination of a Gibbonesque historian, and certainly no evident sociological force lodged in a puny band of outlaw Christians. So too with the modern survival of the Jewish ideal born in Jerusalem almost 3000 years ago. And so was it with the sunny humanness of the Angkor smile in the desolate Garden of Buddha of the twelfth century A.D. The greatest heights of culture and civilization were always fashioned, not within the molds of sociological cause and effect, but within a transcendent vision, and crowned with its leavening effects.

And whenever such a vision occurred it was not a matter of imagination, of pictures in the mind merely. It did not wait upon hindsight. It was no daydream or night fantasy, no seer's musings and no philosopher's theorizing. Rather, it was action and always a new—sometimes seemingly instant—reality: the quicksilver transformation of North Africa, the Near East, and Eastern Asia into the cohesive Muslim world of the eighth century A.D.; the fever of Maoism running through 700 million Chinese in 1949 and affecting them with a strangely alien color that frightened the rest of the world.

It used to please the self-confident rationalists of the eighteenth and nineteenth centuries as a mental plaything to speak of the "great stages in man's evolution": in some way or other, they assumed, the great religious systems— Hinduism, Buddhism, Judaism, Christianity, Islam— were "evolutionary steps" toward a "higher synthesis." This was an entertaining, artificial, and grossly misleading mental perspective that did not emerge either from the systems themselves or from the data but from a basic presupposition of its fashioners; and it did great injury to fact and ignored the precepts of thought made into law by the rationalist thinkers themselves. It was a flimsy sociological mirror of the anthropological theory of evolution, and equally ignorant of its own requirements of empirical evidence.

If, like Sherlock Holmes, we leave aside the fond but unproven assumptions of those earlier analysts and approach the dominant traits of the historical visions from a fresh vantage point, we perhaps glimpse the bare etching of a total picture. When you examine the innards of each Castle vision in history, a clear antinomy emerges. They have a nonconnective history, on the one hand; no one of them derives from the other; and no one is one step better, so to speak, than a previous one. On the other hand, taken together, they integrate a quasi-total picture of the human Castle ideal. A unity emerges, not as if one evolved from the other on a gradualized and improving principle; but as if each one depicted one facet of a superior paradigm, some holistic picture, of which each historical vision was a piecemeal reproduction. It is as if, metaphorically speaking, matter and flesh and mind have been a prism through which the light of that paradigm has filtered and been fragmented into separate rays.

Occasionally a stray mirror of the whole appeared: John the Divine writing about the Adoration of the Lamb; the medieval Sufis discoursing ecstatically about the Bright Pavement of Glory; the Jewish Daniel describing the Ancient of Days above primeval forces and beneath the penumbra of Yahweh; the burning messages of Teresa in Avila. But such was rare. More usually, each vision had a unity of meaning in view of that whole, as the different and separately found colors have a unity in the whole rainbow; while separately they do not constitute that whole, each one implies the whole for its own completion and for its meaning.

Muslims envisioned the utter nearness of spirit. Jews consecrated the visit of the divine to a human world.

Byzantines encased that divinity's light in worldly frames. Romans evinced the source of personal permanence—to be greater than one's human self. Khmers caught the smiling happiness of transformed humanness. Maoism intuited the inviolability of that human self. At Wittenberg, they reclaimed the dignity of human reason. And in Peru, Indiana Plus, men and women made the only known covenant in history with that humanness (they called it the Union) as an open-ended avenue to the infinite perfectibility of that human self.

In each case, the visionaries seem to have traveled light years from their former condition. But it was not time subtracted from life; rather it was time above the usual allowance, seasons when they grew like corn in the night. Their desires were released from the narrow alleyways to a broader rhythm where self blended in harmony with all other things. And the place where they lived became, as commentators used to say of Prairie Avenue in Chicago of the early 1900s, "the sunny street that held the sifted few." The self, no longer an invader of the unknown, a mortal knocking aimlessly at the door of divine mysteries, was at home in a world become a protean and malleable thing for the vision.

And each time, their world was adorned: the Muslim arabesque, the Gothic spire, the Byzantine mosaic, the temple tiers of Angkor, the shooting finials of Peru, Indiana Plus. Yet, while in each and every one you can discern the character of the visionaries' substance, all this meaning and significance did not emanate from things. To parody Rachel Carson, one did not first love a stone, then a dog, then a tree, then a person. There was, first of all, a love of the love which made stone, tree, dog, and person possible and lovable. And this was the talisman of the visionary: you invested the world with what made you human, thereby humanizing it.

But with time and in time, each vision seems to have fallen short of its own ideal. At best, some seem to have arrived at a modern brink point. Because of that, we are presented today with a picture of puzzling and stunted reality. Inheritors of great visions eschewed and still eschew even a relational unity. Officially at least (for it is generally the people who lead the visions to their brink choices and beyond; and it is often the official leaders who scramble protestingly behind the led), there is still *the* Community of Believers, *the* Chosen People, the *one* true Church, the *All* of all things, and so on. At least six of the great visions expanded into professedly religious systems— Buddhism, Judaism, Christianity (Roman, Byzantine, Protestant), and Islam. Each one of the six embedded an exclusionary principle in its outward structure and inner persuasions. At certain early stages of materialization, this exclusivity and conviction of chosenness seemed to be the hinge of strength. It gave cohesion. It inspired.

And each time, the exclusionary principle seemed itself to be rooted in a covenant—sometimes explicit—that the visionaries made with the land on which each vision blossomed. However the visionaries came to it, the land became central to the working out of the vision. Arabia was the altar of Islam for the Muslims; Angkor was the center of the universe for the Khmers; Greece was the Holy Mother for the Byzantines (as was Russia for the Russian Orthodox); Europe was the world for Romans; for the Jews, Jerusalem and Israel were the chosen place of Yahweh's residence; and the New World was the New Canaan for the first American Protestants.

"Land" in each case was not merely the earth men walked upon, but all that was involved as physical and material elements in the land's definition: its waters, stones, metals, and rocks; its contours; its plants, insects, birds, and animals; its smells and sounds, its light and its darkness; the sky above with its changing face, and the sun which rose and set on that land were conceived as belonging, as having been appropriated, to that land.

Thus the land became sacred: each place in it assumed a thousand shapes for the vision. Each moment of the land's time made its own unique statement about the vision's promise. The vision became rooted in that land and was expressed in images and terms of the land by the individual as he talked, thought, hoped, lived, and died on it. Each, vision and person, appeared as an extension or continuation of the land. Each individual as a participant in the vision was an articulation of the land and was intimately connected with it in his human identity and activity.

Yet, today, when you revisit the various epicenters of those Castle visions in order to assess what happened to them in the time since their original moments, you find it is that exclusionary principle incorporated, as it were, in a particular land which has largely determined their parlous condition today. The covenant each made with the land preserved them, surely, for a long time; but it did so by narrowing the optic of their consciousness. Cultural presuppositions bolstered inner convictions but then came to be taken as those convictions. Intangible ideals of vision became identified with political and sociological levers of power. The trees were taken for the wood. And all the trees outgrew the visions.

And so in revisiting each of these places, even while you celebrate the inner light that burst and blossomed there, you hear a threnody of regret and of helplessness sung now by voices without tones. When the land of Angkor disappeared beneath the flood of invaders, the Castle vision of the Smile disappeared beneath, leaving mere monuments. The Constantinople vision appears to cower in a historical crevasse without an exit: once its land ceased, visionary Constantinople retired to insular monasteries; and an irredentist clergy, forever mindful of past political power, continuously decreases and diminishes in prestige and popularity. Islam, expression of the Mecca vision, either is being slowly throttled to death or rests on a gamble: it is being undermined by Arab Socialism (as in most Muslim countries), or it trembles at a fateful crossroads as in Saudi Arabia where a deliberate effort is being made to revivify but "modernize" it. The Jerusalem vision lingers still as an ideal, but clinging to a new, non-Biblical sociopolitical structure (Israel). The lights are slowly dimming and going out around the Roman vision, as the structure ossifies here and there dissolves in a now alien world. The inheritors of Wittenberg find that their passionate logic and personalism has led to possible suicide.

In this day and year, participation in a past vision of the Castle is impossible for us in particular. We were not there when the vision came. And the vision's time is gone and irretrievable. But even to understand what happened is difficult for us. Today, in our majority we are fact-ridden children of a science-oriented and technology-minded world, at the receiving end of a ceaseless rain of innovations affecting everything we do and see and think. Our reaction is an empiricism remarkable for its naïveté: every empirical effect we know must have an empirical cause we can know empirically; anything of vision and of spirit being, as we are taught to say, abstract and nonrational does not belong to real knowledge.

Yet we are humbled even intellectually by the achievements and realizations of Castle visionaries. And this is especially true as regards the Achilles heel of our modern civilization and the knowledge it accumulates with such avidity. That Achilles heel is the human self. Every Castle vision exalted it. But every step we take forward seems to whittle away one more layer of its substance. Within the coded labyrinth of our factual modern lives, there is no place for the unseen and unmeasurable self as substantial reality. Indeed, some would say it has already been liquidated; yet, although it is by now only a phantom idea for some, most of us insist in stubbornly increasing numbers that human life is dehumanized and not worth living unless that self is secure and integral. Indeed, it is precisely the jeopardy of that fully human self that begins to preoccupy us now in literature, art, politics, and religion.

Our official and publicly approved understanding of our selves (i.e., the expert explanations given us of our selves) is absolutely dichotomous. One part, we say and presume, is rational: it rests on verifiable evidence and logical conclusions and is the really noble part of us as human beings—what biology, psychology, sociology, history, and our other sciences tell us. And every acceptable understanding of the self is expressed in psychophysical terms. Another part, we are all persuaded now, is irrational. It erupts in emotions, evades the links of logic, and is less humanly noble but alas an inescapable part of us humans—that which issues in our loves and hates, our mysticism, our religion.

And so we have arrived at a point where we accept a topsy-turvy view of the human self and of the world in which that self must live. It must be a human world, we say, and not an aggregate—however embellished—of matter. But we propose to humanize it only by factual knowledge. "Drat!" we say in the paling shadow of a B. F. Skinner, "the self must be expanded, enriched, made immune to all that nonsense. Let's get a good rational fix on it now." And in myriad ways, we proceed to deny that self any egress or expression other than those we can measure and quantify. We try to give the "irrational part" a meaning from brute facts. We align it willy-nilly with psychophysical norms. We trace its "roots" into the "subconscious" and the "unconscious." Love is defined in terms of sexuality, rather than sexuality in terms of love. Morality is defined within the terms of legal justice, rather than legal justice in terms of morality. Life and afterlife are judged by physical death, rather than physical death by life and afterlife. Humanness is defined in terms of psychological acts and sense-experience; yet, they only derive their meaning from humanness. Male and female are distinguished by the genitalia or, if we are sophisticated, by hormones; but merely to distinguish by chemistry and physical forms is not to give meaning.

But all this quantitative thrashing about does not help us. We silence the instincts of the self. We unknow a primary knowledge. So the self signals its survival by inducing a pain in our minds and a malaise in our wills. We become highly toxic, always liable to fear and mistrust, never far from anger and anxiety. We are rarely confident practitioners in the business of living. At some point, things seem to go out of control; and we slither without warning into a slow descent toward old age and mystifying death. For we have accepted an inner mythology which has measurable dimensions but no transcendent, and presents no ultimate mysteries as windows to the limitlessness beyond the limits of measure. We are given only puzzles to solve; a world of facts glued together by the "consciousness" of "knowing," "informed" people.

And so empirically successful has this unabashed empiricism been that ours appears to be the first time in known history that we can begin to speak of mankind's empirical "consciousness" on a wide—even international—scale. But we must distinguish three levels of consciousness in the sense we are using here. One is most explicit, evident, and available. Indeed, so available is it that its most impressive characteristic is its sustained flow. It knows no night and no day, neither cessation nor decrease. It echoes continuously and almost universally through a web of worldwide communications, a system of network systems which every day spreads more intricately within and between countries, on land, through air and stratosphere. By television, radio, Telex, telephone, computer, wire service, newspaper, news agencies, films, music recordings, periodicals, books, lectures, conferences, universities, schools, tourism, legislatures, churches, foundations, international agencies for trade, finance, industry, science, medicine, and politics. In aggregate, what one might call the "knowledge business."

The consciousness involved on this first level is primarily a factitive one whose voice gains an electronically impressive redolence. It is the purveyed consciousness of its own directors, managers, and producers: telecasters, radio announcers, journalists, commentators, writers, teachers, professors, lawmakers, governments, theologians, philosophers, preachers, theorists, lecturers, travelers, financiers, traders, industrialists, PR men, advertisers, economists, psychologists, scientists. As the directors and messengers of this burgeoning knowledge business, they create a new reality and then preside over and protect it. For them, the message is the medium. The theater of their interest and the point of their concentration is perforce what is most easily and with best effect transmitted by the medium: the physical and the quantifiable—what is visual, audible, smellable, touchable, tastable, and the most immediately "usable." In the end, the system is self-reinforcing; and, finally, the excellence of their media and the degree of their success depends on the heightened sense of sight, sound, taste, smell, and touch. In these sense experiences, it is the form and the structure, not so much the content, that stand as criteria of truth and fact—of "reality."

The second level is articulate and explicit only by way of repetitiousness. A vastly greater number of people participate on the second than on the first level: those who are the due objects of what the messengers on that first level produce (facts and opinions). Reality on this level is what appears in print, is seen on television, or is heard over the radio. To be real and factual, something—anything—must come to them through one or other of the various media. They, too, have been persuaded that the medium is the message. Activity and interest reside increasingly in psychophysical actions as elicited, produced, molded, and guided by the media. And, concomitantly, it is the materiality of men's world and of this universe which crowds in upon them to provide the substance of their judgments, the nourishment of their hopes, the interpretation of their loves and hates, the solution of their difficulties, and, most fatefully, their norm of humanness in themselves and their definition of the human reality.

It is a common persuasion of ours that these two levels of international consciousness adequately if not accurately represent the most deeply human state of consciousness: a web of clear and distinct concepts tied to words and sentences and numbers to describe facts. With these two levels at our command, we can deal very nicely with certain other vast shadowy areas called the subconscious and the unconscious. And, within them, we can get a grip on almost anything. For instance, a new sector with a new name: the parapsychological, two of whose activities are called telepathy and telekinesis; and parapsychologists have a name (the quark) for the subatomic unit of energy in this sector and a method (Kirlian photography) of tracing its activities.

At this level, there are few of us who are not tantalized: surely, we are getting to the core of things; we become anxious to read more, know more. But every question, we soon find, gives us only a fact. And we are surprised that all we can do with that is to ask another question. Soon we recognize mystery metamorphosed by the alchemy of science into a puzzle that makes the labor of Sisyphus look like a quick and diverting warm-up. We begin to glean that the two levels of consciousness together with their sliding panels of subconscious and unconscious are not human in themselves; nor are they the magic crucible in which the meaning of humanness resides. Within the explicit complex of words and the quantifiable activity of bodily matter, there is no meaning for human life. Any attempt to know meaning at this level is the crux of our act of unknowing.

For meaning comes only from a third and deepest level. It has no subconscious or unconscious penumbra. There we use no concepts. Words are superfluous. Our activity there is not traceable along subatomic tracks. Its energy does not issue in any form of ESP. It does not deny facts; but facts are ultimately ratified with meaning only there. And it is at this level that more and more people are glimpsing the new vision of the Castle.

This third level of consciousness, the deepest possible to humans, is the proper domain of the self and the matrix of its humanness. We do not know it by any image or concept or logical process, nor does it operate by any of these. We cannot subject it to any quantification. Each one of us is conscious of it indirectly and only as an abiding presence surrounding our thinking, our feeling, and our doing—in Dylan Thomas' phrase, as "the force that through the green fuse drives the flower."

We can never be sure that our words and actions reach the self in others. But, while we pass through the multifarious elements of our world, as William James wrote to his wife, "a man's character is discernible in the particular mental or moral attitude in which, when it came upon him, he felt himself most deeply and intensely active and alive. At such moments, there is a voice inside which speaks and says: "This is the real me!"

This unaware awareness through which meaning flows starts when, past a certain moment of childhood, we begin—fleetingly at first—to catch glimpses of meaning as distinct from facts but making those facts human and appropriately ours: a smile is more than a widening of the mouth; a handclasp is more than flesh on flesh; a phrase conveys more than the dictionary sense of the words; the body of a dead man is more than a cadaver; a sunrise is more than the end of night darkness.

Thus, facts crowd into us in throngs; but the meanings discerned by the self come only in quick flashes. While we move along the material continua of space and time together with their factual contents, the self is not concerned with facts as such, or the interrelationship of facts, but with the meaning of all facts. Its function is not to elucidate meaning out of facts, but to create meaning for those facts. This it does, not out of its innards like a spider spinning a web from its entrails (nor like the Idealists' man who "thinks it all up"), but by responding to spirit as it shines through the materiality of the universe. And thus the self harmonizes the physical surroundings of man placing all his limits within an illimitless paradigm of light and melting all his rigid particularisms in a universal flow and flux of being.

And so the framework of our humanness slowly emerges from the twilight of infancy and the mists of childhood as a physical continuum over which glitter the bodiless stars of spirit. We never acknowledge it, perhaps. No matter. We depend on the meanings discerned by the full unamputated self in order to make our psycho-physical actions—conscious, subconscious, unconscious—specifically human: to make our eating a celebration, our copulation an act of love, our judgment of other humans morally just, our attachment to one land patriotism, our friendship for another reliant on trust and not proof, our living now valuable for the future, and our dying worthwhile.

While we feel and act and live within the bounds of matter, we become transcendently human, as does our world. Like a tincture of bright scarlet dropped into a glass of crystal-clear water, the meaning supplied by the integral self is to us incontrovertibly precious, manifestly personal, wholly transforming. And, from time to time, perceiving this, we acknowledge its unique value, saying that "we are truly living," "it is good to be human," and "life has a meaning."

Increasing numbers of men and women today find such acknowledgment impossible in modern surroundings. In fact, the cry on all sides is that "we are being dehumanized and our world is being rendered uninhabitable." This is not merely disgust at the mechanical and the systematic, and not simply a pernicious nostalgia. It is rather that already for them a vision of the new Castle casts glints on the horizon of the spirit. It cannot—as it should—invest their full psychophysical life, becoming the atmosphere of their knowing and the light in which they live and act on the world around them. It is cut off by the pervasive thrust at unknowing that encases modern knowledge. Yet without it, there dawns the clear and painful sense of being less than human. The self in us begins to withdraw, to revolt, to stand back from all that makes us unknow the vision. It is just so that we become dislocated from our surroundings, being every day more and more compelled to seek a means by which the self and the light of vision can again invest life with human meaning.

On every side today, we notice this dislocation. People are standing back from the systems of our human living.

They are no longer immersed in and flowing with it willingly. Rather, they stand over against it, as people caught
in its toils and subject to its conditioning. They participate
in its political, economic, social, and religious structures
only by necessity. Nationalism and its first cousin, patriotism, are losing their former hold. The state—originally
the organ of the one and guardian of the other—is "out
there" in an appositive stance to the people; and neither it
nor its operatives, the politicians, get the same respect as
before. One's own economic status is seen as dependent on
the economic system by force of circumstances, but not as
one facet in a mosaic of cooperation in a commonwealth of
goods and services; success takes on new contours and is
wrested from unwilling sources; one survives or flourishes
despite the system. Continually under erosion are all communal molds of social life: the family, male and female
sexuality, the community, the character of public celebrations, community honor and instincts. People stand back
from religious institutions and see them more and more as
aging monoliths with which they share no deep abiding
sense of values and enthusiasm. They maintain the buildings for rituals they wish to see preserved. They see the
institutions as obstacles to progress and problem solving.

But such withdrawals are only some among many
symptoms of the dislocation. Our difficulty lies in our
reading of those and other such symptoms. We count the
millions of copies sold of *Jonathan Livingston Seagull* or *The
Last Days of the Late Great Planet Earth*. Booksellers and
public alike wait for the next wave, the next enthusiasm,
to hit. When it comes, we may all marvel at the public
relations involved, but miss the inexplicable will of millions who seek meaning in the myth of talking gulls and in
mystical tracts about the spirit of good and the spirit of
evil. The record-breaking box-office queues for *Love Story*,
The Godfather, *The Exorcist*, and *Jesus Christ Superstar* will be

explained as everything except eruptions of the self in ever-growing numbers of us groping for the lost dimension of the self, the intangible transcendent. So also will we judge esoteric groupings (Jesus People, Children of God, Processeans, Satan cults, communes, neo-Buddhists, Black Muslims), regroupings (the Traditional Church of Gomer de Paauw, Jews for Jesus, Charismatics, Gay Liberation, Female Liberation), social eruptions (Black Liberation, Symbionese Liberation, prison revolts, Indian revolts, Young Lords), and whatever seem to be fracturing departures from our traditional fabric of life (communal sex, open-ended marriages, flag burning, student apathy, sundered family unity).

We have not yet noticed in all this dislocation the signs of human implosion. We seem not to see a progressive clearing of ground as if for something new to be built. Yet all the things by which we have known our world for generations are changed or changing. The mortar binding the building blocks of our society is chipping and blowing away before a wind of changing spirit that is taking with it too our own accustomed inner landscape. Our own human dimension is changing. And it was a very fast thing. Within our shores and beyond them, there is no country, no city or town, no institution of major importance, that is as it was five years ago.

Even in relatively stable prosperous areas such as America and many countries of Europe, the general symptoms of dislocation are already evident. But over large areas of the earth, particularly in the so-called Third World, the dislocation is more frightening. Great masses of people in Africa, Asia, and Latin America are now held together in reasonably workable units only by the force and pressure of military regimes and governments or beneath the minatory umbrella of a superpower.

It is to these masses in particular that the Pekin vision

of Mao Tse-tung speaks relevantly. Mao has spoken to millions concerning the inviolability of the human self, of the human person as an inner being, of the unlamented miseries which have been inflicted on that person through history, and of the primal force—their response to the vision—which is now working in the masses and will eventually break all the chains including those of the Communist Party in China and elsewhere. We would misunderstand Mao's vision if we limited it to what *we* know of China's history: i.e., that the lot of the majority of men and women from the earliest times has been that their persons belonged to another and a stronger one. That each was a Forbidden Palace: possession of himself by himself was denied; occupation by the other was the rule. This is all true. But Mao's vision includes one new element: the now mounting response of those masses. Without response no new vision is fired. Nothing we do can ultimately conquer that response. But nothing Mao has done necessarily assures it.

The Pekin vision, response and all, hangs on a strange brink. It is locked by Mao's doing—his past doctrinaire cruelty and his dialectical stupidity—within the steel-strung meshes of Marxism-Leninism where all knowing again is reduced to the psychophysical; there is no admitting of a transcendent view. While he lives, he can—as he is now doing yet again—provoke cultural revolution after cultural revolution. He has said that there will be even ten, twenty, thirty, or more of these before his vision is freed from the tentacles of elitist politics. When he dies, there will be only the response of the masses to break those chains apart. As Alexander Solzhenitsyn wrote: "Only the unbending human spirit taking its stand on the front line . . . can be the real defender of personal peace . . ." And only time will tell if the vision Mao has glimpsed in his intuition of the self will be strong enough to escape from the grip of Mao's own Marxism and from the control of a Communist elite, to build itself into social and political institutions which will make the new Castle in Pekin a tangible reality.

The vision of Peru, Indiana Plus issued in that turbulent but almost mystical entity, the Union, incarnated in the states and the Constitution; its antecedents were rooted in a sense of the hand of divinity itself guiding human events within that Union. Where Mao's intuition stopped short at the primal force resident within the masses (his Marxism-Leninism assured this break point in his realization), the intuition of the early visionaries in Peru, Indiana Plus went further—because freer—and embraced the transcendent. Bit by bit, decade after decade since its founding, the Union has roiled and boistered its way down the generations shredding each successive one of its cultural, religious, and political particularisms and localisms, resolving all complications into the ever-rushing lines of spirit. Now, close to its bicentenary, the Union has become so intangible to our psychophysically oriented mentality that many declare it dead, dying, evanescent, a dream that was never real, or a sociopolitical framework sustained only by the rule of law.

But they have forgotten or they never knew or could not express that the Union was primarily a covenant with the humanness of men and women, with the self in each one compacted with all the others, to seek always the best (therefore ever-changing) habitat for the human self in all its variations. This meant and means that progress for the Union implies "the ultimate compassion," as Abraham Lincoln put it, a constant straining and sieving of all the dyes by which the self has been colored in the past and in other regions of the earth, so that the Union could receive and nourish as its own all men and women regardless of color, creed, race, economic misery, or cultural degrada-

tion. That "compassion" today has manifested implications and refinements never formulated before and which
affect such fundamentals as patriotism, cultural differen-
tiation of the two sexes, economic hierarchies, and religious institutional dichotomies. And there will be others.

As Mao in the East raises his last cultural revolution,
the West squints and blinks through the microscope of its
own empiricism to magnify its little knowledge. In the
twilight of this culture and the only civilization we of the
late twentieth century have ever known, many will continue to arrange human affairs according to the "clear and
distinct ideas" of abstractive knowledge gained solely by
empirical means. According as meaning and the understanding of meaning diminish, and merely the functions of
systems take over, the dislocation gap will widen and
widen between the systems and their managers, on the
one hand, and the mass of the people, on the other hand.
People will move less and less according to the set pace;
like Herb Alpert's bossa nova beat, no matter what
rhythm is played, the dancers will never have a comfortable hold on each other.

We cannot say it will be sooner or later. But, without
much warning and as it were by the way, the assemblers
of facts, the manipulators of systems, and the manufac-
turers of psychophysical realities will be seen and will see
themselves as a clamorous minority feverishly dialoguing
among themselves on the outer edges of a new human condition born to sight and touch without their having realized it.

The new condition will be primarily inner to each one
of its participants and mutually shared by them all as a
group—or so we must assume; for so it has been with earlier and different Castle visions. But the particular landscape of the new vision will, we must guess, be as new
and unexpected—as unforetold by what precedes it—as

that of each Castle vision before it. And the road to it may be rougher than that to any other vision. We can guess at some hallmarks of its newness in two ways. We can underline for ourselves the main thrust of the various dislocating events today; for through such irreversible dislocations, spirit has always prepared men and women for Castle visions. We can also refer to past visions, noting the essential contribution of each one to human perfection.

The perceptible yearning in the Pekin vision, the pathos of desires in the Third World movements, and the thread of intention to reach wholeness running through disparate happenings in the United States, all three concern the human self. Even with our ignorance of the new Castle in its full reality, we are led to the conclusion that the common thrust is toward a new liberty for the self, a liberty it has not yet known. What Robert Frost wrote explicitly of the visions's beginning in Peru, Indiana Plus is prophetic of its future:

> Something we were withholding made us weak
> Until we found it was ourselves
> We were withholding from our land of living,
> And forthwith found salvation in surrender.
> Such as we were we gave ourselves outright . . .

For us now, the self is unseeable, untouchable, perceptible only indirectly to our consciousness. In the new Castle, it will assume a native substantiality and a new power. And, again, in past Castle visions we can seek analogs which give us a dim idea of what that substantiality and power will be.

The Mecca vision illustrates the vivacious fluidity between individuals which will make each self whole with the wholeness of all, so that each one's integrity is guaranteed by all the others. At Mecca, that fluidity was spirit; and it was divine.

When we intuit the very quick of the Jerusalem vision

and discern the face of Jewish beauty, we form an idea of the confidence experienced by men the moment they see fulfilled their ancient desire that divine comeliness clothe their earth.

We moderns have relegated the self to the "irrational"; it will become the source of a new rationality, and will embrace a knowledge we neglected when we endowed only the empirical sciences and their results with the name of knowledge and wisdom. That new rationality was once glimpsed both in Constantinople's light that gave meaning to all human discourse, and in Wittenberg's dignity of reason that hoped to make all logic soundly human. Now we have only the binary knowing of empirical mentalism and verbal logic. Then our knowing will be of unitary meaning, and our knowledge by participation in that meaning.

The self will not be forced any longer to function in a personal isolation; we will not, each one, be a walking empire of solipsism; human society will not be converted into a rabble of egos wasting the human scene with incalculable errors and the orderless caprices of some three to five billion monomaniacs, each one bent on doing his or her "thing" in a joyless cosmos where personal jeopardy is the condition of societal freedom. We can see the new Castle's counter-values to such degradation in the calm and confident merriment of the Angkor Smile, and in the personal guarantee of immortality in the Roman vision. Surely we must take that Smile as the expression of the guarantee, and both Smile and guarantee as issuing from the bathing luminosity of the new knowing.

The search for the new meaning of the self has already engulfed us all. That new meaning of the self will shrug away the poverty of this age. It will be a reflection of the overall meaning shining around society as a new atmosphere. The naturally spontaneous self-proclamation "I am an I" will mingle with echoes reverberating softly but persistently in the world of Everyman. As the significance which touches it will belong to the invisible reality of humanness, so will its effects be told on each human, on human time, on life-rhythms, and on our world.

But neither significance nor meaning will be our doing. For such salvation comes to us humans only from what is more than human. If we, men and women, were to aim at fashioning a humanly transcendent Castle, it is guaranteed by that very fact not to be transcendent. And the peculiar destiny of humankind is that only by the greater than human can it be human successfully. This is why the form and face of the new Castle will remain unknown to us after all our guesses and all our analyses of past Castle visions. No child can outline the face of its mother while lying in her womb. The new Castle will not be a man-devised combination of systems already known to us; nor will it include a sort of universal religion put together by human hands from bits and parts of past religions and voted into existence by a sum of ayes and noes.

In our desire for the Castle, we cannot perceive what we desire. Nor need we. What we can do is to respond to spirit, not because we are persuaded by logic and not because we conduct successful and conclusive experiments, but because free response to love is the only action typical of the human person. Our material world thus becomes a human universe in which we have been loved all along by a love we never recognized.

ABOUT THE AUTHOR

Malachi Martin, a former Jesuit professor at the Pontifical Biblical Institute in Rome, was trained in theology at Louvain, specializing in the Dead Sea Scrolls and intertestamentary studies. He received his doctorate in Semitic languages, archeology, and Oriental history. He subsequently studied at Oxford and at the Hebrew University, concentrating in knowledge of Jesus as transmitted in Jewish and Islamic sources. He has lived in several of the countries and has spent time, both over the years and again within the past year, in all the additional countries where the Castle visions of this book appeared and developed. Dr. Martin is the author of *Jesus Now, Three Popes and the Cardinal, The Encounter, The Scribal Character of the Dead Sea Scrolls* and *The Pilgrim*, and numerous articles for magazines and journals.